PICARDIE

Anvers

PAIS BAS

ESPAGNOLS

FRONTIE...

Cologne

Rhin

Tilsle

Amiens

Soisson

Rheims

Mayance

Francfort

D'ALLEMAGNE

ISLE DE
FRANCE

CHAMPAGNE

Sedan

Spire

Paris

Metz

LORAINE

Strasbourg

Troyes

Nancy

Chartre

BEAUCE

Sens

Basle

Orleans

Bezancon

FRANCHE COMTÉ

BOURGOGNE

...rges

Dijon

BERRI

Nevers

SUISSES

Zurich

Moulins

Chalon

Macon

BOURBONNOIS

Geneve

Lion

SAVOYE

NIVERNOIS

Chamberi

ITALIE

Clermont

AUVERGNE

Vienne

Grenoble

le Puy

Cahors

Rhodes

SEVENNE

DAUPHINÉ

Milan

ROUERGUE

Alès

Rhone fl.

Valence

Milhaud

Viviers

Turin

Genes

...ouse

Nismes

Orange

LANGUEDOC

PROVENCE

...rbonne

Monpellier

Avignon
Aix

Toulon

Frejus

Nice

Golfe de
Lion

Marseille

Mer Mediterranée

Orient

50

45

TREASURES
OF
FRANCE

EDITIONS
MOLIÈRE

TREASURES
OF
FRANCE

FOREWORD
DENIS TILLINAC

JEAN GALL
SUZANNE MADON

TRANSLATED BY
DEREK JOHNSTON

FOREWORD

On land tamed by many generations of farmers, France offers the historian, the lover of beauty and the stroller an unparalleled range of architectural splendors. This book is testimony to the genius of the West and to one country's richness from the Roman era to the present day, via the Romanesque, Gothic, Baroque, Renaissance and Classical.

The author opens his superbly illustrated account with the Christian sources of an art that developed in the footsteps of the disciples of St Martin: monasteries, churches and cathedrals. In France the least little valley has its squat bell tower or elegant spire, symbols of a Catholicism highlighted by the country's place names. This is the "sweet France" of piety and chivalry celebrated by Charles Péguy, the France of saints immortalized in stained glass windows. Built in the early Middle Ages, the châteaux have evolved over the centuries, from small feudal forts to sophisticated manors to the gentlemen's residences of a declining aristocracy. This is the France of the knight, of the man of honor: home to the good life whose sheer diversity points to an enormous mix of architectural influences. As Elie Faure has put it, France lies at the crossroads between the misty north and the sunny south; and the result is a complex harmony in which human longing and the quest for the absolute are reconciled.

Yet this book would not do justice to the soul and the poetry of France if it did not take us into its villages. Villages sometimes found in austere, even wild settings, even though the greater part of the country's landscapes have about them the "gentleness" dear to the poet Joachim Du Bellay.

The French reader of this book will discover treasures he knew nothing about; while readers from other lands will feel themselves summoned to travel, to go off the beaten track into an enchanted world where the Germanic, the oceanic, the Latin and the Flemish come together as undying sources of inspiration.

Denis TILLINAC

CONTENTS

THE MARCH OF THE NATIONS OF EUROPE TOWARDS THE CHRIST

14TH CENTURY FRESCO OF ST PETER THE YOUNGER, STRASBOURG

ABBEYS AND CHURCHES

THE PRE-CHRISTIAN PERIOD

Their meaning is enigmatic, but megaliths could be connected to pre-historic religious practices. According to Flaubert Carnac "has caused more foolish things to be written than there are stones on site", yet it is the most spectacular of locations. Built between 5000 and 2000 BC by a little known civilization, it has several burial mounds, hundreds of menhirs, the tallest rising to seven meters, and dolmens which are sometimes decorated with symbolic designs.

Some menhirs were later marked with the effigies of roman gods, others crowned with a Christian cross, like that of Saint-Duzec, on which were also sculpted the instruments of the Passion. These cut stones are also found in the south in Aveyron, in Languedoc, in Provence, even in Corsica; at Filitosa the menhirs are sculpted in human form and date from the middle of the second millennium BC, the figures bear arms.

The Celts, later the Gallo-Romans, have left many signs of a wide variety of religious practice. Their sanctuaries are scattered throughout every region of the country; we have figures of deities in stone, bronze and brass. The god of Euffigneix, in Haute-Marne, wears the characteristic Celtic torc, as does that of Bouray in Essonne. Celts and Gauls venerated nature, certain woods for instance; water in particular, witness the many ex-voto offerings at the sources of the Seine and at Chamalières.

The Nautes pillar found beneath Notre Dame in Paris was set up about 40 BC and shows both Gaulish and Roman deities who evidently coexisted peacefully for many years. Rome refused to tolerate the druids because they were too influential politically, but the new temples were often built on traditional sites. So Nîmes, where the Maison Carrée was built in the reign of Augustus, owes its name to a water sprite. The Alyscamps in Arles, a huge Gallo-roman burial site, will for centuries also be a Christian cemetery. The site had become sacred and many people living far off wished to be buried there.

BETWEEN LEGEND AND HISTORY

The Emperor Constantine, by recognizing Christianity in 313, ended the period of Christian persecutions. The Church will soon be organized with little regional variation. The country is divided into dioceses administered by bishops whose seat, the cathedra, gives us the word cathedral. Cathedral originally meant a collection of places where the bishop carried out his spiritual and temporal duties: near the church, which is increasingly impressive to emphasize the presence of religious authorities in a city, we find the bishop's residence, a palace, for instance at Albi; buildings where clergy are trained, where the poor are taken in and looked after, for the bishop is responsible for them too.

The monastic movement, which started in the East, spread to Europe. These communities were often mixed, (Jouarre for example which dates from the Merovingian period,) men and women were later separated, we are not sure when. Chapels, churches and convents flourish from the fourth century on, particularly under the influence of St Martin of Tours. The story is well known: Martin was a Roman legionary who cut his cloak in two to clothe a beggar; Christ appeared to him shortly afterwards and Martin set out to travel the country preaching the gospel. He was for a while bishop of Tours, built the first monastery in the country at Ligugé, then at Marmoutier. Many notable personalities were converted, chapels and monasteries were built, and their institution was often connected with miraculous events, which in turn gave rise to pilgrimages that continued for many centuries.

The Archangel himself supposedly told Aubert, bishop of Avranches, to built a church dedicated to him; he built the Mont-Saint-Michel. Nine hundred years later, at Sainte-Anne-d'Auray, the mother of the Virgin Mary appeared to a ploughman, The cathedral of Notre-Dame du Puy was also built following appearances of the Blessed Virgin, while Holy Trinity Church in Fécamp was built on the site of a monastery where from the seventh century on a few drops of the Christ's Blood were miraculously preserved in a casket.

Many foundations were thank-offerings: a Crusader returns home safely from the Holy Land or a major epidemic has ended. Such buildings were often built to relieve a guilty conscience. Nicholas Rollin, chancellor of the Dukes of Burgundy, gave a part of his huge fortune to found the hospice at Beaune at the end of the Hundred Years War. The magnificent Hôtel-Dieu is a model of Flamboyant Gothic style and reflects the astonishing power of the Duchy in the days of Philip the Good. Such foundations are often linked to the histories of religious orders, which were founded, reformed, or even disappeared over the·years.

THE GREAT RELIGIOUS MOVEMENTS

In the sixth century St Benedict of Nursia laid down at Monte Cassino the rules adopted by most western religious orders: monks, under the authority of their abbot, spend their time in prayer, manual labor and intellectual effort. From 910 on the Abbey of Cluny will play a major role in the spread of the Benedictine movement. The church choir is surrounded on three sides by an ambulatory giving access to radiating chapels. This building with so many altars reflects a growth in the cult of relics and the pilgrimages accompanying it. Benedictine abbeys and priories take root all over Europe, especially in Italy, where the movement began and the order flourished.

Late in the eleventh century Robert de Molesme founded the Abbey of Cîteaux in reaction against the splendors of Cluny. Bernard of Clairvaux will soon take up the Cistercian ideal; the desire for simplicity is seen in the unadorned architecture of the houses he founded. Cistercians were famous for clearing uncultivated land, often settling in wild and inhospitable places that they then made fertile. Seven hundred monasteries for men and nine hundred women's houses were founded in Europe and in the east over a period of two centuries. Alongside this movement we see the appearance of Trappists, leading a life of contemplation and silence.

In 1084 St Bruno and his companions settle in the Chartreuse mountains near Grenoble thus founding the Carthusian order. The choice of an isolated place and the way the buildings are laid out display the monks' desire to be alone even as they live in community. Amongst many others, the Abbey of Bec-Hellouin, founded in 1034, is an example of how monasteries throughout the Middle Ages were centers of cultural activity and the exchange of ideas. A great theologian, Anselm of Aosta, came to teach there, while its abbot Lanfranc later became Archbishop of Canterbury.

After the Crusades and the setting up of the States of Jerusalem, orders of monk-knights such as the Templars and the Knights of Malta are founded to shelter and protect pilgrims going to the Holy Land. Begging orders appeared in the thirteenth century and Franciscans, Dominicans, Carmelites and Augustinians, in the Cistercian spirit, condemned the spectacular wealth of certain houses. St Francis of Assisi founded the Order of Friars Minor or Franciscans in 1209. His followers made a vow of total poverty, and originally begged for their living. The fact that they wore a belt of cord won them the name Cordeliers; they would later be called Capuchins from the long hood (capuchon) they wore. St Clare, the sister of Francis, soon founded a contemplative order for women, the Poor Clares. St Dominic's brothers dedicated themselves to preaching, particularly in cities, where they vied with the Franciscans in founding new houses.

In the mid thirteenth century, Robert de Sorbon, confessor of St Louis, founded a college in Paris for theological students; its fame would be wide indeed. For many centuries the highest religious authority, next to the Pope, would be the Sorbonne. The Pope would live in France from 1309 to 1377. When the Bishop of Bordeaux was elected Pope Clement V in 1305, Italy was plagued by troubles that led the Pontiff eventually to settle in Avignon. John XXII, who followed him in 1316, started work on the Papal palace. Benedict XII would turn it into a fortress, duly enlarged between 1342 and 1370 by Clement VI, Innocent VI and Urban V. Few palaces are bigger or more sumptuous than the Palace of the Popes. It still contains today many masterpieces of medieval art, for example the wall paintings of the Stag room and the ceiling decorations of St Martial's chapel.

St Ignatius Loyola founded the Company of Jesus in 1540. This order, distinguished for its rigorous theological training, will assume the duty of defending the Counter-Reformation following the Council of Trent. It was particularly active in the training of clergy and the education of young people in colleges famed for their excellence.

At the same time the Carmelite movement, which had many years previously been brought to Europe by hermits from Mount Carmel in Galilee, took on new life inspired by St Teresa of Avila.

In the sixteenth century the Lutheran Reformation led to schism within the western church. The Wars of Religion ravaged the country from 1562 to 1598, when the Edict of Nantes, ratified by Henry IV, re-established freedom of worship for Protestants and restored the goods confiscated from them. Ten percent of the population of France was now Protestant. This century is also marked by two important calendar changes. In 1563, the first day of the year is changed from the 1st of April to the 1st of January. This ended a period of change and confusion. The Julian calendar, established by Julius Caesar, was reformed in 1582 by Pope Gregory VII. To make up for the divergence between calendar time and solar time that had increased over the centuries, they jumped from 4th to the 15th of October.

The seventeenth century saw an explosion of new religious orders: Lazarists, Oratorians, Visitandines… In 1685, the Revocation of the Edict of Nantes led once more to the persecution of Protestants, marked by the history of the Camisards in the Cévennes. Certain regions witnessed a very high rate of emigration. A century later it is the clergy who in turn are victims of persecution by the Revolution. The Church's property was nationalized, religious communities dissolved, monasteries dismantled, churches stripped and pillaged. After the Revolution Dom Guéranger at Solesmes and Dom Muard at La Pierre-qui-Vire revived the Benedictine communities. The religious movement struggles to get back on its feet, while at the same time anticlericalism is on the increase. Finally, 1905 sees the separation of Church and State. The story of places of worship is not however over: we see Matisse work on the chapel at Vence and the building, right in the middle of the twentieth century, of the cathedral of Évry.

THE BUILDERS' ART

Romanesque art, with many regional variations, developed in a constantly evolving society; from the eleventh to the early thirteenth centuries, the great period of monastic growth. Historians no longer distinguish it as fully as they used to from the Gothic style that gradually replaced it. The two names were conferred much later. An architect from Normandy, Charles de Gerville, used the term Romanesque for the first time in the early nineteenth century. Amongst its finest examples are Fontenay, Saint-Pierre in Moissac, Royaumont, Saint-Bertrand-de-Comminges, Saint-Sernin in Toulouse, the Chapel of Berzé-la-Ville or Sainte-Foy in Conques.

Examples of Gothic art include the Abbey church of Saint-Denis, the cathedrals of Sens, Senlis, Noyon, Paris, Laon, Angers, Poitiers, the church of St Mary Magdalene at Vézelay, the Abbey church of Pontigny. A second wave of cathedrals includes Bourges, Chartres, Reims, Amiens, Beauvais, Meaux, Rouen, Bayeux, Coutances and Auxerre.

We see the style change in Troyes, Tournai, the Sainte-Chapelle in Paris; it becomes High Gothic in Metz, Clermont-Ferrand, Narbonne, Rodez, Albi or the Jacobin church in Toulouse. Finally the Abbey of the Mont-Saint-Michel, Trinity Church in Vendôme, the collegiate church at Cléry, the Abbey church of Saint-Riquier, the churches of Saint-Nicolas-de-Port, Saint-Gervais in Paris, Saint-Pierre in Caen, Saint-Nicolas in Troyes are all examples of Flamboyant Gothic style.

All these places from cathedrals to simple chapels, display the talents of builders, but also of glassmakers, sculptors, goldsmiths and tapestry weavers. The glassmakers contribute to the magic of the place by playing with light, as at Chartres, Saint-Séverin in Paris or at Notre-Dame in Évreux: all wonderful examples of fourteenth century stained glass. Naval carpenters will sometimes construct their vaulted ceilings like ships' hulls; wood carvers create masterpieces like the choir stalls at Amiens, the rood screen at Saint-Fiacre, the glorious roof-beam at Lampaul-Guimiliau. Here the Calvary surrounded by a great crowd displays the stone carvers' art. See those at Plougastel-Daoulas or Notre-Dame in Tronoën, the oldest one we still possess. Funeral monuments will reach the highest peaks of achievement at Saint-Denis and at Champmol, near Dijon. Stone workers will create church doorways, tympanums and cloister capitals all in stone yet looking like lace, fabulous and realistic figures in Strasbourg, Chauvigny, Autun or even the Smiling Angel at Reims.

Goldsmiths will create wonderful reliquaries and liturgical objects, skillfully working the precious metal: the treasure at Conques is a magnificent example. Tapestry weavers will adorn walls with coverings like the Apocalypse in Angers. Painters will engage all their talents as in the chapel of the Templars at Metz or at Notre-Dame-la-Grande at Poitiers.

Ceaselessly restored, reconditioned, improved, the ancient heritage of the country will still add surprising places to its store as the twentieth century progresses. Just visit the chapel at Ronchamp, by Le Corbusier. Matisse will spend the last years if his life decorating the Rosary chapel at Vence, Cocteau will leave his mark on Milly-la-Forêt and in 1996 Mario Botta's cathedral was dedicated at Évry.

"Architecture is a journey", said Le Corbusier. Our religious heritage illustrates this thought better than any other. From city center to country lane, we see development and transformation in both art and faith, periods of vigor alternating with moments of torment, the temptations of splendor and the desire for a more rigorously honed spirituality.

THE CONSECRATION OF A CHURCH BY A BISHOP

SAINT-BERTRAND-DE-COMMINGES

THE BASILICA

It was a Roman site where, in 72 BC, Pompey built the city of Lugdunum Convenarum on the road to Spain, southwest of Toulouse. Lugdunum quickly became a busy city, but it declined following the collapse of the Empire. An early Christian basilica in classical style was built there in the early 5th century; the Visigoths destroyed both it and the town in 585. Gregory of Tours claims that they slaughtered the entire population, did not leave one stone standing on another and burned the ruins. He seems to have exaggerated; the worship of the basilica was never interrupted. Lugdunum became the seat of the bishops of Comminges. In 1083 a young man was appointed to the see; he was Bertrand de l'Isle-Jourdain, and was the grandson of the Count of Toulouse. With extraordinary energy he rebuilt the city, constructed a Romanesque cathedral on the foundations of the basilica, performed miracles, real ones: fifteen in all, and was canonized in 1222. His tomb became a place of pilgrimage and the town took the name of St Bertrand-de-Comminges. Another churchman was especially important for the town; Bertrand de Got, archbishop of Bordeaux and elected Pope, as Clement V, on the 5th June 1305. He was the first of the Avignon Popes. In 1307 he requested that the romanesque building be pulled down, (the bell tour still stands) and a huge gothic cathedral be built in its place to hold the crowds of pilgrims visiting the tomb of St Bertrand or on their way to Santiago de Compostela. It was St Mary's Cathedral and can be seen in the middle of this photograph.

In the foreground is the Basilica of St Just de Valcabrère, built, probably on the site of the old Roman burial ground, with Roman tombstones and stone from a nearby Roman villa; it is a sober building, resembling classical Roman basilicas.

SÉMUR-EN-BRIONNAIS

THE COLLEGIATE CHURCH OF ST-HILARY

Geoffrey V of Sémur may have had a great name but spent his days careering around Burgundy with blackguards of his ilk, plundering, kidnapping and terrorizing the locals. One of his great-uncles was St Hugh, Abbot of Cluny, another had granted lands to found a convent for "noble ladies", at Marcigny; one of his aunts had been the Prioress there.

Geoffrey's actions were so scandalous that he even stole from the nuns at Marcigny. Then his uncle Hugh had a word with him. We don't know what was said, but Geoffrey repented and built the collegiate church at Sémur between 1125 and 1130.

The east end is particularly fine: observe the play of the rooflines of the apse and apsidiole chapels, they all have different heights and are dominated by a superb octagonal bell tower. FOLLOWING PAGES

ORCIVAL
THE BASILICA

It is normal for the choir of a church to face east; the people come in from the west. The basilica of Orcival is hidden deep in the Baroquette valley and clung up against a mountainside. You come in from the south.

It was built of local volcanic stone in the 12th century, hence its dark gray color. It is called "Our Lady of Chains", because of the iron chains that ex-prisoners used to hang on the walls as thank offerings after their release. It also has a unique statue of the Blessed Virgin.

It dates from the 12th century and was made of wood covered in silver gilt. It survived the Revolution hidden in the church and seems to reflect all aspects of life: one side of Our Lady's face is smiling, the other is stern.

CERISY-LA-FORÊT
THE ABBEY CHURCH OF ST VIGOR

It was founded in 1032 by Robert the Magnificent, son of William the Conqueror, and building continued until 1087.

It is right in the heart of the Normandy forest. It is a distant descendant of a 6th century religious house destroyed during the Viking invasions which had been founded by St Vigor, Bishop of Bayeux, hence its name. Five of the eight bays were removed in 1811; the present façade was originally the wall of the choir.

Later additions, notably the gothic chapel dating from 1260, barely altered the romanesque look of the building. Looking at the choir we can see the original apse, with its three levels, the fine towers surrounding it, the angled buttresses, the small mullioned windows, the squat bell tower with two levels of old arcades and a level with arched bays.

27

NOHANT-VIC

A FRESCO IN
ST MARTIN'S CHURCH

St Martin's church in Nohant-Vic, George Sand's village, dates from the 11th century. It started as a simple rectangular nave with a similarly rectangular choir. An apse, with chapels was added in the 12th century and the inside of the church was covered with frescoes.

The effect is still striking today, because like many such painted churches, the contrast between the outside light and the paint colors is surprising.

28

On the other hand the paintings are rarely the work of first-rate artists, but of naïve, amateur painters who, supported by faith and imagination, have embellished biblical stories with details, archaisms, transpositions, anachronisms, but above all with really original expressiveness.

What strikes one at Nohant is the faces, almost grimacing with effort, animated gestures, full of life; the simple way they have painted the faces of these round-eyed and red cheeked country folk with their worried looks. This painting of the Last Supper is on the choir side of the traverse wall of the church.

POITIERS
NOTRE-DAME-LA-GRANDE

It is one of the most beautiful façades of romanesque art and a major symbol of the city of Poitiers, yet we know practically nothing about this magnificent church, particularly its early years. It is situated right in the heart of the ancient capital of Poitou, a few steps away from the palace of the Counts of Poitou and mentioned for the first time in a charter dating from 924. What did it look like then? Who built it? When exactly? Nobody knows.

The northern wall is the oldest; the major part of the building dates from the 11th century; the interior has a fine collection of romanesque frescoes and other treasures and its façade is a sheer masterpiece. It was put up in the 12th century, when the nave was being prolonged out beyond the two transepts. It has three horizontal levels. At the lowest level we find three porches surmounted by a (somewhat damaged) sculpted frieze representing a poignant Nativity.

At the second level there are 14 arches containing eight statues of seated apostles, surmounted by four apostles and two bishops, all standing. The latter are St Hilary, the first apostle of Poitiers and his disciple St Martin. The gable which is the third level is divided horizontally by a band; the upper part is marked with a network of lines, the bottom half is circular, showing a sculpted Christ in glory blessing with his right hand and holding a book in his left. Above are representations of the sun and moon together with the symbols of the four evangelists.

SÉNANQUE
THE ABBEY

Three Cistercian abbeys are amongst the jewels of medieval art. Monks from Mazan in Vivarais founded Le Thoronet and Sénanque around 1140. Silvacane had just started to observe the discipline of Cîteaux. Sénanque stands near Gordes and Roussillon, its white buildings with flat-stone roofs beautifully framed by the Vaucluse hills. The abbey flourished for two centuries, acquiring lands, mills, and guesthouses.

Gradually, as was frequent at the time, it abandoned Cistercian austerity. In 1544, it was partly sacked by the local population; the resulting repression brought dreadful hardship to the villages of the Luberon. Numbers dwindled and it was saved by the owner who bought it following the Revolution: unlike many others he restored the buildings. Sénanque also kept its original look: its church crowned by an octagonal dome, its cloister and chapter room soberly but majestically decorated. After many adventures a community settled there once again at the end of the 1980s.

FONTENAY
THE CLOISTERS

Though founded 900 years ago the Abbey of Fontenay is magnificently preserved. In the 12th century St Bernard and his companions settled in the middle of a beech forest.

The community, with ever increasing numbers, erected new buildings on lands rich in springs, the name Fontenay suggests fountains. The abundance of pure water allowed the monks to farm trout and their efforts were much appreciated. Fish even appear in the arms of the Abbey.

The real treasures of Fontenay are, however, the abbey church and the monastic buildings. The buildings, stripped of ornament, very evident in the architecture and decoration here, perfectly reflect the Cistercian ideal: no flourish should take attention away from prayer and meditation. The buildings are arranged around cloisters where the arches are supported by pillars with sober geometric patterns.

34

LE THORONET
THE CLOISTERS

Le Thoronet is a perfect example of the power-struggles that could bring civil and religious authorities into conflict. This abbey dates from the early 12th century, when a few monks left the abbey of Mazan in Ardèche, and settled near Tourtour and then at Lorgues. In the 13th century, there were twenty professed monks living at Le Thoronet, plus ten lay brothers; two hundred years later, there were fifteen; in 1790 seven, all very old. The abbey would have fallen into decay, had it not been for Prosper Mérimée, who, in 1873, restored it to its original romanesque style. Interestingly, in 1290, the Count of Provence ceded his overlordship of the village of Lorgues to the abbey. The injured villagers took a court case that lasted 500 years in order to free themselves from the regulatory authority of the church and in order to regain their former rights and privileges. They didn't succeed until 1698. The abbey was by then in decline, it would close within a hundred years. FOLLOWING PAGES

MOISSAC
THE ABBEY

The Abbey of Moissac remains one of the great Benedictine examples of romanesque architecture. It was founded in the 7th century, flourished under St Odilon, the Abbot of Cluny, who in 1047 gave it a new dynamism when he incorporated it into his congregation. Moissac then founded a string of daughter houses and, being very well known, attracted crowds of pilgrims as they wended their way to Santiago de Compostela.

It suffered great damage in various wars and at the Revolution; it was almost knocked down to make way for a railway line in the 19th century, but the plan was thankfully abandoned. The old abbey church of St Peter has a portal dedicated to the Revelation of St John, which is amongst the great treasures of romanesque sculpture. The church combines romanesque and gothic elements: the romanesque in stone, the gothic in brick. But the cloister is perhaps the most impressive part; it has seventy-six arches over fine pillars with superbly decorated capitals. There are floral motifs, fabulous animals and biblical figures.

VAUCELLES
THE ABBEY

Once the monks library, but since destroyed by fire, this building, with its empty windows and broken walls bears all the signs of the endlessly repeated wars since its founding in 1132.

The Hundred Years War, the war of the "Écorcheurs", the Franco-Burgundian War, the Franco-Imperial War, the Thirty Years' War, the French Revolution, and two World Wars: each time the abbey was pillaged or sacked or razed or burnt.

40

It was as if the faults of its founder had indelibly marked it since its foundation: Hugues II d'Oisy had long been a violent, irascible, unscrupulous man when, on 16 March 1131, he met Bernard de Clairvaux, who persuaded him firstly to cool his passions and secondly to provide land for a Cistercian monastery.

Today, however, only four rooms survive: the superbly vaulted monks' room; the auditorium, the only place where speech was allowed; the chapter house, completed in 1175 and the largest in Europe; and the sacred passage, where monks and choristers donned their hooded robes before entering the church to sing the holy office.

VALENCE-SUR-BAÏSE
THE ABBEY OF FLARAN

Near Condom in the Gers department, the Cistercian Abbey of Flaran was founded in 1151; it was a daughter house of Escaladieu in the Pyrenees. It is a set of buildings built in a beautiful garden on the site of a 5th century Roman villa. Traces of mosaics have been found in the basements and foundations. But the Abbey suffered so many misfortunes that everything of any importance that survived bears the marks of those troubles.

Protestants destroyed parts of the cloisters during the Wars of Religion, during the Revolution the monks were dispossessed and the buildings sold; it was then used as farm buildings up until 1970. It was finally bought by the Gers county authority; partially destroyed by fire in 1972, it needed extensive restoration work. A 14th century romanesque gallery remains from the cloister. The romanesque abbey church has a three bay nave with side aisles, a transept, a semi-circular ambulatory with apsidiole chapels.

The refectory, dormitory and monks' cells occupy the upper floor. They met in the chapter house, which is seen here with its remarkable proportions and ogival ceiling. PREVIOUS PAGES

VÉZELAY
THE MYSTIC MILL

This Basilica is dedicated to St Mary Magdalene. She was the sister of Lazarus, whom Jesus raised from the dead. It is an absolute masterpiece of Romanesque architecture. It was built in 1050, rebuilt a century later following a fire, given gothic additions, ruined by the Revolution and by lightning, restored and more or less rebuilt by Viollet-le-Duc in the 19th century.

Everything in it is worthy of admiration: its site on top of a hill, its air of spirituality, the architecture, the sculptures, its unbelievable artistic richness. Of all the carvings at the tops of the pillars, the one portraying the Mystic Mill is the most famous, combining mysticism and symbolism and biblical echoes with everyday life. Abbot Suger described this scene, and had it represented in stained glass when he built his basilica at St Denis.

It is a simple, everyday, rural scene. On the left a man is pouring grain into a mill, on the right another is filling a sack with the flour. What makes it unique is its symbolic meaning: the first man is Moses who represents the Old Testament, the second man is St Paul and represents the New Testament. The mill wheel is placed in such a way that the sun always falls on it no matter what time of day it is. It symbolizes Christ transforming the old law given by Moses into the new law preached by St Paul.

UZÈS
FÉNESTRELLE TOWER

In Uzès in the Gard you find the only example in France of a round bell tower. It is so named because it has so many windows (fenêtres).

Built in the 12th century, it has five stories above a windowless ground floor. It is all that remains of the romanesque cathedral which was destroyed by Protestant armies in 1563, during the wars of religion.

The previous church, built in 1090, had been destroyed during the Albigensian war. St Theodorit's cathedral at Uzès was rebuilt in 1652 and the Fénestrelle Tower was preserved. It is no longer a bell tower; you can admire it from afar, but not visit it.

BEC HELLOUIN
ST NICHOLAS' TOWER

Like all religious institutions in Normandy the Abbey of Bec Hellouin suffered many reverses, in particular during the Hundred Years' War and the Revolution. It was founded in 1304, destroyed and rebuilt several times. St Nicholas' Tower was once the abbey belfry, built in 1467 to hang four huge bells.

They were probably too big for an apparently fragile building: the nave collapsed in 1591 and was never rebuilt. The abbey already had a ring of six smaller bells. All were taken down and broken in 1791.

The Doorways were knocked and replaced by a 17th century classical façade. The Anglo Norman style tower was 36 feet in diameter and 197 feet high: it is now lower as the lantern at the top caught fire in 1810. It was replaced by a balustrade with eight statues including the Virgin Mary and Saints, Andrew, Michael, Benedict, James, John and Nicholas.

ST MICHAEL'S MOUNT
THE ABBEY

The Celts imagined this little island surrounded by thick forest to be the abode either of the dead or of the gods and called it Tomb Mountain.

In 706, St Aubert, Bishop of Avranches, was led by a vision to build an oratory there dedicated to the Archangel Michael.

In the tenth century the Duke of Normandy handed care of the site over to twelve Benedictine monks from St Wandrille, thus founding the Abbey of St Michael's Mount. The mysterious vision of St Aubert caused it to become one of the main pilgrimage sites in France. During the Hundred Years' War the village was fortified; nearby Tombelaine Rock was captured by the English in 1423, but the Mount was never seized.

The Revolution expelled the monks and used the buildings as a prison. In 1874, it was classified as an historical monument and underwent major restoration.

Today, standing amidst a huge expanse of sand the granite island is covered by the village and crowned by the abbey some eighty meters above sea level. You enter by passing through the ramparts, through a succession of courtyards before climbing the Grande-Rue, lined with medieval houses, amongst them "Logis Tiphaine" where Du Guesclin is said to have placed his wife in safety before leaving for the wars. Steps and terraces allow one to admire the facades of the abbey church and the "Merveille", that part of the monastery where gothic art is displayed in all its glory.

CHARTRES
THE CATHEDRAL

To really appreciate the cathedral of Chartres you must admire it from the plain of La Beauce where, to quote the poet Péguy, it rises out of an "ocean of wheat". This is how, ever since its consecration, pilgrims arriving in their thousands to honor the Blessed Virgin, have first glimpsed it.

This master-piece of gothic art is built over one of the biggest crypts in France, all that remains of the Romanesque building destroyed by fire at the very end of the 12th century, as are also the towers and the western façade crowned with the royal doorway, delightful statues carved out of the pillars about 1150. After the fire the building was quickly rebuilt. It was completed in 1220 when St Piat's chapel was finished; this now houses the cathedral treasury. Later, in the early 16th century, the northern tour would be given a flamboyant spire in which we can already glimpse the coming Renaissance style. Its builder, Jean de Beauce, would also build the screen around the choir.

Chartres is also famous for a collection of exceptional stained glass windows, miraculously preserved since the 13th century. The artists in stained glass have displayed all their talents for us in a symphony of color and a veritable Bible in pictures. One of its jewels is the great rose window where the Virgin and Child sit enthroned in glory. There is a profusion of scenes: the Jesse Tree, an iconographic theme that first appeared in the 12th century, retraces Jesus' genealogy; also rose windows with the story of the Passion.

STRASBOURG
THE CATHEDRAL PORCH

There are many things to admire in Strasbourg cathedral, but the central doorway in the west end is the best. It was planned by the architect Erwin de Steinbach and is part of a project that was never finished. When he died in 1318 they added another story that was to sit between two towers, but only one was built. Seven hundred years later you still feel that something is missing.

Then you see the lacelike, elegant carving in pink sandstone, spreading out vertically, a veil full of geometric figures, interlaced and intermingling. The carved figures are magnificent: in the tympanum you see the last moments of Christ's life on earth, from the entry into Jerusalem to the Ascension.

The cathedral was built between 1252 and 1274 in gothic style with both French and Rhineland influences. The façade was built between 1277 and 1399, the spire from 1399 to 1439.

BAZAS
THE CATHEDRAL NAVE

Bazas is today a modest community in the Gironde, barely 4000 inhabitants. Did it once play a major role in the history of Aquitaine? If it didn't, how did it come to have such an imposing cathedral? How come it was consecrated by Pope Urban II who in 1096 preached the first Crusade here?

The present gothic building was built in 1233. It survived the wars of religion and the Revolution. In 1561 Protestants took over and sacked the town, they threatened to knock the cathedral down in 1568. In 1789 revolutionaries pillaged it, cut the heads off statues, threw the most sacred relic, a phial with a few drops of John the Baptist's blood, into the latrines.

Why this rage? Perhaps because, for three hundred and nine years (1340 – 1749), bishops of Bazas shared temporal power with the seneschals and provosts of the King. FOLLOWING PAGES

PARIS
NOTRE-DAME

Photographically speaking, this is the most interesting of the facades. Not because it is more beautiful than the others – Notre Dame is a splendid cathedral whichever way you look at it – but because the triple protection afforded by the river, the iron fence and the garden mean it cannot be looked at from close up.

The rose window is especially striking: each of its twelve central segments gives rise to two others, the three combining to form yet another large, pointed segment. Above the window, a Gothic gable takes up the same motif, while below it the ornamentation on the door of St Stephen recounts its subject's martyrdom: his capture, his trial before the Sanhedrin and his stoning to death.

Unfortunately this door, too, cannot be inspected from close up. The spire rising above the intersection of the nave and transept is a 19th-century reconstruction by Viollet-le-Duc: like many other features of the cathedral, the original was destroyed by the revolutionaries of 1789.

ROUEN
THE "CROWNED TOWER" OF ST OUEN

There is nothing on earth like the Butter Tower of Rouen Cathedral unless it's the "Crowned Tower" of the Abbey Church of St Ouen, also in Rouen. The two buildings soar into the sky and are but a few dozen yards apart, both are in the same flamboyant gothic style, have the same elegance, the same finesse. They were built in competition: the first demonstrated the power of the bishop, the second that of the Benedictines. We draw no conclusions from the fact that the second is over twenty feet higher than the first… nor from the fact that the central tower of the cathedral is twice as high!

What we are forced to admire in the Crowned Tower is its daring and its transparency. You can see the sky through the stone. The tower base is on a platform that is square at the level of the church roof, but becomes octagonal higher up; there are four corner towers, also octagonal, each topped with a dome and a stone cross. The tower itself ends in a crown of pinnacles, whence the name Crowned Tower! It was built in the early years of the 16th century, but oddly enough we know little about its building, its architect or how it was financed. Its rival, on the other hand, owes its name to its sponsors.

St Ouen church belonged to the abbey of the same name, founded in 558 by Clotaire II; it was destroyed several times, even more frequently rebuilt. The oldest parts of the present building date from 1318. It was severely damaged during the Revolution. The monks' dormitory (18th century) has become the city council chamber; the building has belonged to the City Hall since 1800.

AMIENS
THE CATHEDRAL

Viollet-le-Duc called it "the perfect gothic cathedral". One hears only praise for this place of worship and, on visiting it, sees only marvels.

Here you see the roof vaulting: the cathedral was built to raise the eyes to hope and light. It is 144 feet high, almost as tall as St Peter's in Rome. Until Beauvais was built in 1288 it was the tallest in France. It was built with simple diagonal vaulting, except for the crossing that also has ribs and strengtheners: it is the oldest example in France of this type of building. It is supported by 126 thick pillars, but they are finely decorated; in particular note the capitals. It is the biggest and brightest cathedral in France with clerestory windows and 41 tall windows. FOLLOWING PAGES

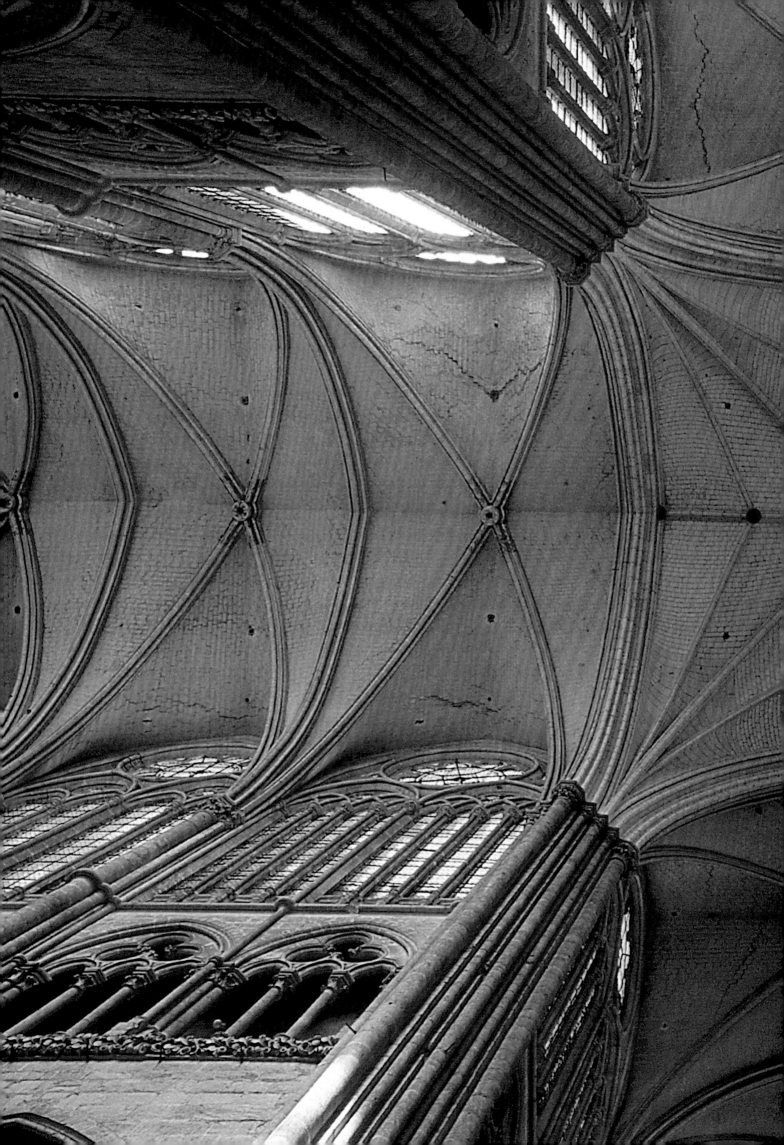

BEAUVAIS
THE CATHEDRAL

Few buildings have experienced such a troubled history, such lofty ambitions or such costly damage as Beauvais Cathedral.

It was built to replace, on the same site, the cathedral destroyed by fire in 1225; the remains of the old nave still exist. But work was very slow: it took forty-five years to build the chancel: twelve years later it collapsed.

It had scarcely been rebuilt when the Hundred Years' War broke out: Charles the Bold attacked the town and damaged the cathedral. In 1499 it was decided to rebuild the nave, but this plan was abandoned fifty years later in

favor of a spire over 490 feet tall, this was finished in 1573. Beauvais Cathedral was now the most beautiful, the tallest, and the brightest cathedral in Christendom. This state of affairs lasted a mere six years. During divine service on Ascension Day in 1573, the spire and three stories of the tower collapsed: luckily only slight injuries were suffered by two members of the congregation.

In the 17th century work started again on the nave, only the first section appeared above ground. It was wrecked by 18th century revolutionaries but managed to escape the 20th century incendiary bombs raining down on the town.

No gothic building is higher: 159 feet.

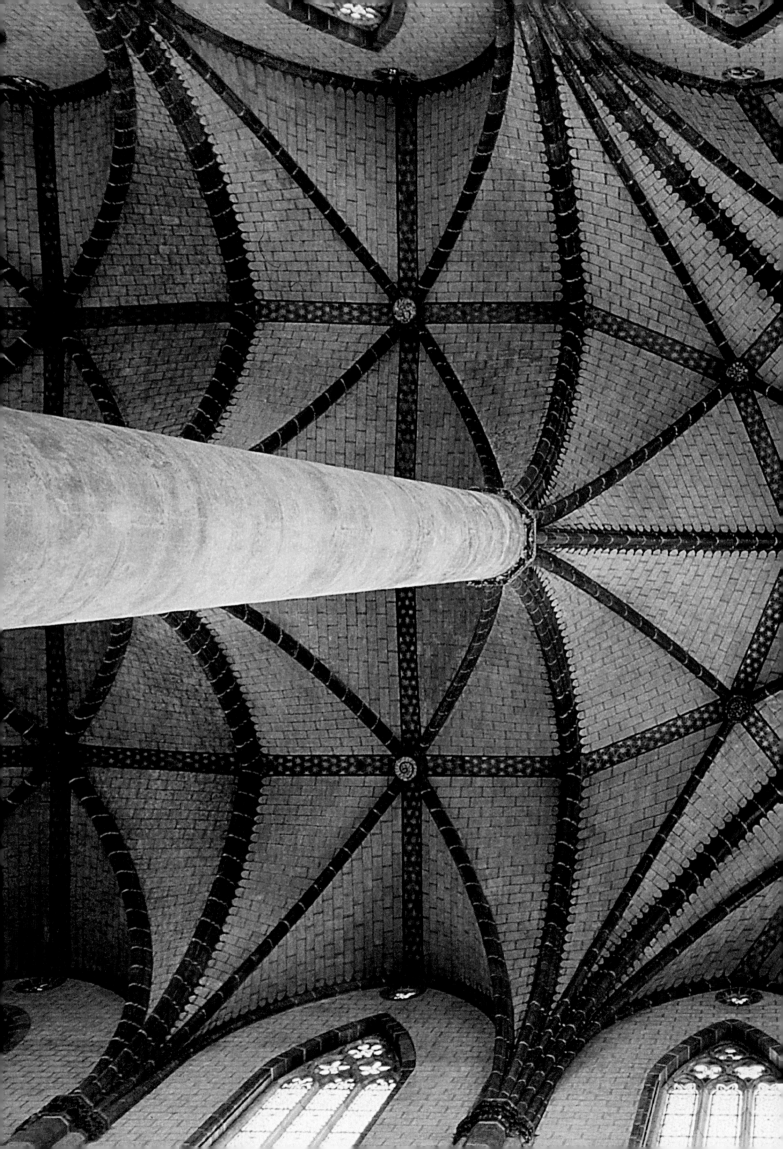

TOULOUSE
THE JACOBIN CHURCH

This original building, called "the palm tree" must be seen! It was built in brick in the 13th and 14th centuries and like many Dominican churches has two naves, separated by a row of six pillars supporting a 72-foot high roof with diagonal vaulting.

A 7th pillar, in the same line as the others but 8 feet further east supports not only the arch of the apse but also the first vault of the nave.

This pillar bears the weight of 11 keystones, 12 vault ribs and 11 strengtheners. You get the impression that the vaulting is turning around the pillar and this feeling is accentuated by the colors: brown for the ribs and ochre for the brickwork. PREVIOUS PAGES

REIMS
ANGELIC SMILES

Clovis, the first Christian King of France, was baptized in this cathedral, built in 1212. From Louis the Pious in 816 to Charles X in 1825, 24 Kings of France were crowned here. During the First World War 4600 shells fell on Reims (12000 out of its 14000 houses were destroyed).

The cathedral remained standing but required twenty years work to restore it. It has 2300 statues; this is the most famous, the star of the collection. It is the guardian angel of St Nicaise and stands to one side of the left-hand doorway in the façade. It was carved between 1211 and 1500.

It has always been singled out as exceptional; in Christian iconography, you rarely see an angel smiling! Stranger still, on the right-hand side of the central doorway of the same façade another statue shows the Angel Gabriel who is also smiling, and even more so! They are so alike people often mistake one for the other. Yet many details are different, but the evidence is there; in Reims there are two smiling angels!

ALBI
ST CECILIA'S CATHEDRAL

This powerful ship-like building has an austere exterior in pink brick that hides the splendor of its internal decoration: a flamboyant rood screen, wall paintings and decorated vaults.

Bernard de Castanet, Bishop of Albi, started the building shortly after his appointment to the see in 1282.

The building work here went hand in hand with that of the Bishop's Palace, La Berbie, which also looks like a citadel rising up on the banks of the Tarn. A bare forty years after the burning of Montségur, which ended the merciless fight against Cathar "heretics", one can see how determined he was to assert the all-powerfulness of the Catholic Church.

Today La Berbie houses the Toulouse-Lautrec Museum. The artist was born a few yards away in the du Bosc residence and lived for a long time in the family castle of the same name, in the country to the north of Albi.

The city, which boasts splendid old houses around the Saint-Salvy cloisters, is also the birthplace of two intrepid travelers: La Pérouse and Pierre Benoît, chiefly known as the author of the novel *L'Atlantide*.

BOURGES
THE CATHEDRAL STAINED GLASS

Bourges cathedral is the exact contemporary of Chartres: also begun in 1195, also in pure gothic style, also possessing exceptional windows. The oldest stained glass in Bourges dates from the primitive romanesque cathedral, destroyed in 1195, but little survives.

However the 13th century windows illuminating the choir on three levels are perfectly preserved. The colors are bright and the way gothic builders played with light is here a resounding success.

This example shows coopers at work and commemorates one of the three guilds (the others were the carpenters and wheelwrights) that paid for, "sponsored", these masterpieces. The scene is taken from a tall window telling the story of the patriarch Joseph, son of Israel, sold by his brothers, but now an important official in Egypt. PREVIOUS PAGES

LENTILLES
DER'S CHURCH

Between the forest of Orient and Saint-Dizier, to the north-east of Troyes, an immense reserve was created thirty years ago to regulate the course of the Seine: Der-Chantecocq Lake. In the heart of the Champagne wetlands, the Der region (the name might derive from dervo, the Latin for oak tree) has become a tourist attraction, but migrating birds also stop here, notably the crane.

The surrounding district is home to a series of unusual churches, like that of Lentilles, with its slender tower. This beautiful half-timbered church, it stands in a heavily wooded area, has beautiful examples of woodwork. The villages of Puellemontier and Chavanges also boast houses and churches in the same style. The church at Ceffonds has 16th century stained glass from Troyes, a great glass-making center at the time.

Voltaire lived for fifteen years in this neighborhood at the home of his friend the Marchioness du Châtelet at Cirey-sur-Blaise. Nearer still, Bonaparte was a student at the military school of Brienne.

CAST
QUILLIDOUARÉ'S CHAPEL

The Châteaulin basin, watered by the Aulne, huddles between the Arrée Mountains, the Black Mountains and the Menez-Hom, overlooking the Crozon Penninsula.

A few miles from Châteaulin, whose coat of arms reminds how important salmon fishing is to the town, the little church of Cast reminds us of the patron saint of huntsmen.

In front we see a curious group of sculptures recalling the life of St Hubert, who was called to faith while out hunting. According to legend as he pursued a stag he saw a cross appear between the antlers of his prey.

The church at Cast was built in a region known for pardons or local pilgrimages: Sainte-Anne-la-Palud and the pretty village of Locronan that gives special honor to its patron saint, Ronan. It is part of a string of chapels and churches scattered around the countryside of Brittany, like Sainte-Barbe, Saint-Fiacre, Kernascléden and Loc-Envel.

A holy well, statues, a rood screen, frescoes, a vaulted arch, the very setting… each has its own charm.

LE FAOUËT
ST FIACRA'S CHAPEL

St Fiacra was a monk who originally came from Ireland; he is now the patron saint of gardeners and farmers.

This 15th century chapel in Le Faouët was dedicated to him and built by the well-known Boutteville family, who lived in Brittany. It houses an absolutely magnificent treasure: its wonderful rood screen.

Rood screens were built between the choir, where the clergy sit, and the nave where the faithful gather.

They were often used as a visual aid for teaching the faith, as was the case with this one. Oliver Le Loergan carved it between 1480 and 1492, in the days of Anne, Duchess of Brittany. Here you see the eastern side, the side all the members of the congregation could see. Five ogival arches support a balcony with eleven panels; above we see Christ on the cross with the two thieves.

Beneath there are four statues depicting four vices to be avoided: theft (a man stealing fruit from a neighbor's tree), laziness (a Breton bell ringer), drunkenness (a man is vomiting a fox) and lust (a love scene). It is carved in wood with precision and detail, almost like lace, and brightly colored.

NOIRLAC
THE ABBEY

The Abbey of Noirlac is one of the best-preserved Cistercian foundations. It was founded by a disciple of St Bernard of Clairvaux around 1130, and stands on a backwater of the Cher south of Bourges, near Saint-Amand-Montrond. After the Revolution, a porcelain factory was set up within its walls thus preventing its destruction. The church, its pure lines in the best Cistercian spirit, is flanked by the monastery buildings and 13th and 14th century cloisters.

The builders have skillfully harmonized volume and natural light. Three lancets and a rose window light the east end of the abbey church; no architectural flourishes distract our gaze from the light that spills through them. In the refectory, similar but wider windows have been given 20th century transparent glass: the room has its own lightness.

The chapter house is equally majestic in its simplicity. It opens onto a cloister with delicate openwork and arabesques, gently emphasizing the sobriety of the building.

79

ROYAUMONT
THE ABBEY

Louis VIII requested an abbey be founded after his death. Two years later, the future St Louis and Blanche of Castille started to build Royaumont. St Louis loved this abbey and frequently stayed there.

This important foundation, which was built about the same time as the great cathedrals, sheltered up to four hundred monks. Its Cistercian cloister, the biggest in France, surrounds a French style garden.

The Abbey had varying fortunes, despite numbering Mazarin amongst its abbots. Just before the Revolution an astounding abbot's residence was added. This resembles Palladio's Villa Rotonda in Vicenza. It later became a cotton-spinning mill: the vast abbey church was torn down to provide housing for the workers. Some 13th century buildings have survived, for example the splendid gothic refectory and kitchen, others were remodeled in the 19th century.

In 1923, its owner, Henry Goüin, started to restore the buildings and to transform them into a cultural center. The Royaumont Foundation, created in 1976, has continued his work. Every year it organizes a prestigious musical program, lectures, conferences and residential activities for artists and thinkers.

PREVIOUS PAGES

MARSEILLE
THE "GOOD MOTHER"

Marseille's relationship with the Virgin Mary has been a stormy one. Veneration of Mary arose spontaneously in the early centuries: pilgrims petitioned her when they went up to the chapel on the La Garde hill overlooking the city.

The church was pillaged and shut at the Revolution, its statues of the Blessed Virgin destroyed. In 1804 a priest paid 15 francs for a statue of Mary carrying a scepter, which he replaced with a bunch of flowers, and placed it in the church where it soon attracted the faithful.

During the reign of Napoleon III, church (who saw the site as sacred) and army (who found the site a useful observation post) managed to come to an agreement, so the architect Espérandieu built the present basilica and the sculptor Eugene Lequesne made a statue that he placed on the top of the bell tower in 1870. The statue was soon named the "Good Mother", the protectress of Marseille and its citizens; it is of gilded bronze, is 33 feet high and can be seen far out at sea.

BETHARRAM
NOTRE-DAME CHAPEL

You see a wide baroque façade between two austere square towers: it is the entrance to the Notre Dame chapel in Betharram, ten miles west of Lourdes. This is miracle country, and there was indeed a miracle! The Virgin appeared to shepherds at the beginning of the 16th century (that early!) and the first chapel was built there on the banks of the tumultuous mountain stream of Pau.

It quickly became a popular pilgrimage destination and was replaced, a few years later, by a second and bigger chapel that was burnt in 1569 in the Wars of Religion.

Louis XIII and the Counts of Béarn had a third chapel, in the baroque style, built in the 17th century.

Four big white statues from Louvie-Soubiron, a nearby quarry of Pyrenean marble, decorate the main door: They represent the four evangelists who look like rugged local farmers. In the middle the Blessed Virgin crushes underfoot the serpent of evil and in her arms carries the child Jesus. The interior is decorated in pure baroque style by the painter Bernard Denis (1652-1722) and the decorator Jean Casassus (1679-1776).

PÉRIGUEUX
SAINT-FRONT'S CATHEDRAL

Périgueux and Périgord are named from the Petrocorii, Gauls who settled beside the River Isle. From the river there are beautiful views of the quayside houses in the old part of the city, a trading center from which rises a cathedral whose lines and roof shapes astonish the viewer.

Saint-Front's cathedral was built between the 11th and 12th centuries on the Byzantine model, five domes covering a building laid out in the shape of a Greek cross. The pinnacles were added in the 19th century during huge restoration works overseen by Abadie, future architect of the Sacred-Heart in Paris. This questionable and controversial "interpretation" has however given us a building unique in France.

CASTLES
AND MANORS

FROM LEGEND TO HISTORY

From the eagles' nest at Peyrepertuse to the gardens at Versailles, from the walls of Angers to the jagged roofs of Chambord, the castles of France are enormously diverse. This variety can often be seen in the same building. The Louvre illustrates eight centuries of change from the fortress of Philip Augustus to the pyramid of Pei. The Louvre is exceptional, but the principle is familiar. Every age has not only built its own buildings, but has remodeled famous buildings, adapting them to the style of the day. This process makes any attempt at chronological classification difficult, quite apart from the fact that many owners and builders were not tied down by the period they lived in. Every century had its "wild" builders, like the lord of Roquefeuil building the fortress of Bonaguil, near Cahors, while his contemporaries were building luxurious houses. It was a perfect example of the sort of defensive building put up in the desert against the Mongol hordes. Bonaguil was never once threatened with attack.

Apart from the history of wars and treaties, of important events and quaint stories, these treasures of architecture speak to us of changes in outlook and ways of living, of arts and technologies, of regional differences and sometimes of an individual's dreams. They also became the crucibles where the talents of master craftsmen from different countries were put on show, where they applied new ideas picked up on their travels. Nobles often brought back new tastes from abroad. In the 13th century Crusaders back from the East were entranced by the refinement and comfort they had observed there. So they set out to enlarge their windows and put glass in them, as much for the way it looked as to keep out the cold and the damp. Carpets and tapestries, canopies and curtains decorating beds, had the same purpose.

Powerful nobles gathered artists around them, thus forming artistic workshops. Jean de Berry who built Mehun-sur-Yèvre in 1367 asked the Limbourg brothers to illuminate manuscripts for him. The Dukes of Burgundy also called on Flemish craftsmen and, in the 14th and 15th centuries, they were outstanding in all artistic disciplines. These craftsmen were themselves often widely traveled; they had been exposed to many influences and reinterpreted them into new forms.

The taste for travel observed in craftsmen even affected kings up until the 17th century, but for reasons of security this time, though also because they liked it. Charles VIII resided in Plessis-les-Tours or in Amboise more often than he did in Paris. Francis I often lived in Fontainebleau, and especially in Saint-Germain. Louis XII was particularly fond of Blois. So Benvenuto Cellini, describing how his travels from 1540 until 1545 obliged him to follow Francis I, said he "had to camp with the court in places where there were scarcely two houses. They put up canvas tents, like Bohemians".

From the 18th century on kings became more sedentary. Palaces rose on what had once been hunting lodges, built for a very brief stay, as they went from one lodge to another depending on the fortunes of the hunt. Versailles is a case in point, as is Saint-Fargeau, there are many others.

Versailles, the epitome of classical taste, exemplifies another mindset, that of the Sun-King, whose palace was conceived as a political manifesto where every detail reminded one of the king. Here all had their appointed place in a perfectly controlled over-arching scheme. Kings would later prefer privacy and intimacy; this was why the apartments were changed in the reigns of Louis XV and Louis XVI.

Two names would dominate the 19th century. Prosper Mérimée, Inspector of Historical Monuments, traveled tirelessly throughout the country listing its architectural heritage, which was often in ruins. He was for a while assisted by the most famous architect of the day who became his friend, Viollet-le-Duc, who undertook a vast program of restoration. In particular he refurbished the favorite residence of Louis-Philippe, the Château d'Eu, and in 1860, for Napoleon III, he totally rebuilt the 15th century castle of Pierrefonds.

MEDIEVAL CASTLES

The first fortresses were built before the year 1000, at the time of the Viking raids. They were originally wooden buildings, later of stone; built on high ground to protect a town, guard a road or a waterway. This was why the Louvre was built by Philip Augustus. For centuries, when the country was a mass of small fiefdoms, fortresses were also built to mark the boundaries of a duchy, a province, a territory. Najac, built by the Counts of Toulouse is an example; so is Haut-Koenigsbourg, overlooking the Rhine valley. Cathar castles are amongst the oldest: Montségur. Philaurens, Quéribus or Peyrepertuse. They are astounding buildings reflecting the history of a religious movement which flourished in Languedoc at the end of the 13th century, though most were originally built to defend the frontier between the French and Spanish kingdoms.

Guédelon in Burgundy demonstrates a most unusual approach to medieval castles. The association of master builders of Puisaye has taken up a challenge: building a fortress which is typical of the 13th century using the tools and materials of the time. Since 1997 about thirty quarrymen, stone dressers, wood clearers, carpenters, blacksmiths are working in a vast clearing where, as in the olden days, they find all the materials they need on the spot: wood, stone, clay, water. Medievalists are regularly consulted to avoid any anachronism. By the year 2020 Guédelon should be a perfect copy of the type of fort build between 1250 and 1350, like the fine castle of Ratilly, which is near the site.

Some time after his marriage to Eleanor of Aquitaine in 1154, Henry Plantangenet, heir to the powerful Counts of Anjou, became King Henry II of England. The kingdom of France was at that time a frail force compared to Henry's vast possessions. Although they were returned to France in 1204, these lands would be a bone of contention between France and England until the end of the Hundred Years' War in the mid 15th century. Château-Gaillard, built by Richard the Lionheart on the borders of his Norman possessions in 1196-1197, was many times taken and retaken by the two parties. The Castle of Angers, belonging to the Counts of Anjou, still contains 12th century features which predate the great reconstruction of 1228. Its name is still associated with the famous wall hanging of the Apocalypse, based on the cartoons of Hennequin of Bruges dating from 1375. Henry II and his son Richard the Lionheart both died in Chinon, another symbol of the struggle between the French and the English It was here that Charles VII brought his court in 1427. The king had but a shaky grip over a few provinces and ruled an insignificant kingdom. It was largely occupied by the English and dominated by the Dukes of Burgundy. In 1429 in Chinon, he met the person who would bestow new legitimacy upon him and allow him to be crowned: Joan of Arc. The court was to remain at Chinon until 1450. It was to the castle at Loches that the king brought his favorite, Agnes Sorel. The dungeons of the castle remind you of the cages in which Louis XI used to keep his prisoners.

In 1602 another residence belonging to Charles VII would become the property of Maximilien de Béthune, who had just been put in charge of State finances by Henry IV. From then on he would be known by the name of his estate: Sully. A hundred years later Voltaire would be exiled to Sully for defamatory writings against the Regent.

Louis XI, having spent twenty years intriguing against his father Charles VII, spent the twenty years of his reign trying to rebuild his kingdom. Firstly he had to fight the powerful Duke of Burgundy, Charles the Bold, then his son-in-law Maximilian of Austria who had inherited some of his possessions. Louis XI particularly liked the intimacy of the castle of Plessis-les-Tours, where he died in 1483. However he had already started to rebuild a much more prestigious site: Langeais. Here a few years later Charles VIII was to marry Anne of Brittany and make the Duchy of Brittany a French possession.

In about 1370 joiners and carpenters had split into two distinct trade guilds. Tables replaced trestles, armchairs replaced folding stools, new forms of furniture were becoming fashionable. In the middle of the 14th century firearms and cannon transformed ideas about defense. More barbicans and outer walls were built to hold back assailants who might breech the walls. Dwelling quarters were becoming more comfortable. The keep was from now on more symbolic than defensive: it was the lord's residence, symbol of his power, rather than a military advantage. Bit by bit, right up to the 17th century, the castle would lose its defensive function; it would soon have no military use. The banks of the Loire are a magnificent example of this change. They are dotted with Renaissance masterpieces such as Amboise, Azay, Blois, Chambord, Chaumont, Ussé, Villandry or Châteaudun; others belong to the classical period: Cheverny, Valençay and Serrant.

FROM THE CASTLES OF THE LOIRE TO THE SUN-KING

Charles VIII was born in Amboise in 1470. His reign saw the first flowering of the French Renaissance. The Italian Wars allowed the French to discover the new forms of artistic expression flowering in the Italian peninsula. When he returned to Amboise in 1495, Charles VIII brought back from Italy sculptors, goldsmiths, gardeners and a famous architect, Dominic de Cortone, known as Boccador. Italian influences gradually mixed with French Gothic traditions; they first influenced decoration, then had a more radical influence on how space was used as we see at Gaillon (1502-1509) or at Chambord.

At the same time windows were getting bigger, chimney breasts and rooms were being decorated with stuccowork and gold. From now on great attention would be paid to a new element in ceremonial building: the staircase. It had become an expression of the magnificence and refinement of the building.

Louis XII took on his predecessor's wife, Anne of Brittany, and also his claims over the Italian kingdoms. He liked Blois, where he built a new wing from 1498-1503; his Director of Finances started to build Chenonceau in 1513. When Louis died in 1515, his son-in-law Francis of Angoulême became King Francis I. It was during his marriage that plates were used for the first time in France. That very year Francis I inaugurated his reign by winning the Battle of Marignan, but the Holy Roman Emperor Charles V would win back the province of Milan from him five years later. Francis I would spend his whole life trying to get his hands on Italy. This had the effect of increasing the size of the court and encouraged greater lavishness in the style introduced by Charles VIII. In 1519 the French Renaissance really got going when work started on Chambord; meanwhile Leonardo da Vinci came to live in Clos-Lucé. Francis started work on Fontainbleau in 1528, where he gathered together a veritable school of artists, and undertook the total renovation of Saint-Germain-en-Laye. In either 1544 or 1545, a little before his death, he gave Pierre Lascot the task of transforming the Louvre.

His son Henry II was born at Saint-Germain-en-Laye. As a child he was held hostage in Spain following the French defeat at Pavia. The castle was given to his favorite Diane de Poitiers and Philibert Delorme would build Anet for her in 1545. The wars against the Huguenots, which had begun under his predecessors, got bitterer during his reign, even though he supported German Protestants against the Emperor. When he died in 1559, his Italian ambitions were definitely in tatters, but practically all former English possessions in France were now in French hands. Francis II, son of Henry II and Catherine de Medici, was born at Fontainebleau in 1544. He acceded to the throne in 1559, but died the following year. His brother, the future Charles IX was only ten years old, so Catherine de Medici became Regent. She immediately gave Philibert Delorme, the author of the treatise Building Well at Low Cost, the task of building the gallery at Chenonceau. This architect would begin building the Tuileries Palace four years later. In 1572 the marriage of Charles' sister, Marguerite, to the Protestant Henry of Navarre was followed a few days later by the St Bartholomew's Day massacre. Charles died at Vincennes in 1574 and Henry III became King. Henry had no children, so the probable successor to the throne was now his brother-in-law, who was unacceptable to the Catholic parties. The Holy League was formed in 1576 to support the claims of Henry of Guise. But friends of the king had him assassinated at Blois in 1588. However the king was growing closer to Henry of Navarre, and before he in turn died at an assassin's hand, in 1589, he named Henry as his successor.

Henry IV would only be crowned in 1594, having converted to Catholicism. The Green Gallant had Claude Mollet design the gardens at Saint-Germain-en-Laye. He would sign the Edict of Nantes in 1598 to dampen fervor and he gave Sully the task of restoring the Finances. But Henry was himself assassinated in 1610. His son, the future Louis XIII, was then nine and his mother Marie de Medici became regent, her chief minister was Concini; she gave power to Richelieu in 1624. Louis inherited his father's taste for hunting, but obviously not his passionate nature: his wife would wait twenty-two years before conceiving a child. The future Louis XIV was born at Saint Germain-en-Laye in 1638. Around these castles in which the kings of France liked to take up periodic residence, (until Henry IV at any rate,) factories making cloth, silk and furniture developed. Louis XIV, with Colbert's help, would rationalize them all. Fortunes created following the discovery of the New World enriched Spain and Portugal first of all, but also had an effect on other European countries. French artists and craft workers were particularly appreciated south of the Pyrenees and trade flourished.

FROM THE SUN-KING TO NINETEENTH CENTURY GOTHIC

Young Louis was five when his father died in 1643. His mother Anne of Austria and Monsieur, the dead king's brother, were officially regents; they worked with Mazarin, a former assistant to Richelieu, who had taken over from him. Mazarin was close to the Queen Mother, legend has it that he was her lover, and quickly drew down on his head the hostility of powerful men in the kingdom. Saint-Simon used to get worked up about the cardinal's "vile and foreign origins" and how he could "persuade the king that every person of high birth was his natural enemy and that, to manage his affairs, he should employ persons of no quality". A parliamentary revolt, followed by a revolt of the nobility, (the Fronde,) gripped Paris, forcing the young Louis, his brother, their mother and Mazarin to flee the capital for a while in 1649. When the cardinal died in 1661, Louis XIV decided not to replace him: he would reign as absolute master. He started to organize the "tools" of his power and commenced gigantic building works at the little castle his father had built at Versailles. He installed his court there in 1682 and imposed a form of etiquette where every courtier had a precise role.

Helped by Colbert he would found academies of science, music and architecture, paying as much attention to artistic detail as he gave to the government of his kingdom. Fouquet's castle Vaux-le-Vicomte played a decisive role in the conception of the Sun-King's Versailles. The Great Condé's Chantilly was another source of inspiration, particularly the gardens and the fountains which were the work of Le Nôtre. Versailles would henceforth be a model which many would try to imitate, Louis II of Bavaria for example. The gardens of Versailles would be the scene of many memorable public occasions, all to the glory of the sovereign. Even the approaches to the Palace are a statement of his power, with their vast parade ground from which three avenues fan out, the center avenue being the widest in France, even wider than the future Champs-Élysées.

When Louis XIV died in 1715, having reigned for fifty-four years, his great-grandson came to the throne at the age of five. Following the regency of Philip of Orleans and his double, Father Dubois, Louis XV took power at the age of sixteen. He would stamp Versailles with a new art of living. He created many private apartments, instead of places to see and be seen. He built the Petit Trianon in the gardens for Madame de Pompadour. The Petit Trianon would be Marie Antoinette's favorite spot; she remodeled its surrounds in accordance with the latest taste recently arrived from England. Instead of wide, open spaces, built to impress the visitor, smaller rooms were preferred; instead of formal beds and lawns, cunningly organized disorder flourished, imitating nature in ways made fashionable by Rousseau. It was a sort of miniature paradise with clumps of trees, little valleys and tree covered walks.

The Revolution emptied most castles of their furniture and their decorations. They had become public property and were dispersed, pillaged or sold. But the Empire and the Restoration quickly took up the task again.

In 1803 Talleyrand acquired Valençay, a castle which had famously belonged to John Law. In 1808 Napoleon had King Ferdinand VII interned there when he placed his own brother Joseph on the Spanish throne. The emperor had asked the Duchess of Chevreuse, the owner of the castle of Dampierre, to be his jailer, but when she refused she was exiled. In Compiègne, which he had completely restored, Napoleon met his second wife for the first time. (Joséphine had retired to Malmaison, where Bonaparte had frequently stayed and where he had written the Civil Law Code.)

During the Second Empire Compiègne became one of Napoleon III and Eugenia de Montijo's favorite places. They organized luxurious receptions there and the guests were offered all sorts of entertainment. Mérimée composed his famous dictation for such an occasion. The emperor soon wished to restore nearby Pierrefonds and gave Viollet-le-Duc the task. He had already restored Vézelay and the citadel at Carcassonne. At that time the castle of Charles of Orleans, which had been completely renovated at the beginning of the sixteenth century, had been abandoned for over two hundred yeas; it had been bombarded and pulled down under Louis XIII. The architect thought at first he would rebuild the keep and leaving it surrounded by "romantic" ruins, but ended up restoring it from top to bottom. For thirty years he worked on it, giving free reign to him imagination: this "restitution" was in fact an interpretation of the original model, a sort of hold-all of medieval style, part historical reality, part personal inspiration and desire to adapt the buildings as a place of retreat and relaxation fit for an emperor. The resulting astonishing and controversial building gave us the phrase "Pierrefonds gothic". Coming after the fashion for neo-classical buildings, the neo-gothic style took its inspiration from English trends and was widely copied. Twentieth century architects would be more rigorous, striving to restore buildings to their original state. A difficult task nonetheless, for it assumes that one can freeze a single moment of what was, after all, a continuous development.

Today it is estimated that about one thousand royal and aristocratic buildings are part of the French architectural inheritance. They bear witness to the efforts of about forty kings, each wishing to add his stone to royal residences. Aristocratic families did likewise, themselves imitated by well-off middle classes. Many reveal sumptuous surprises: furniture, objets d'art, tapestries, historical documents... old stables, various annexes, at the heart of which we find gardens and formal parklands which are themselves pieces of a past teeming with stories.

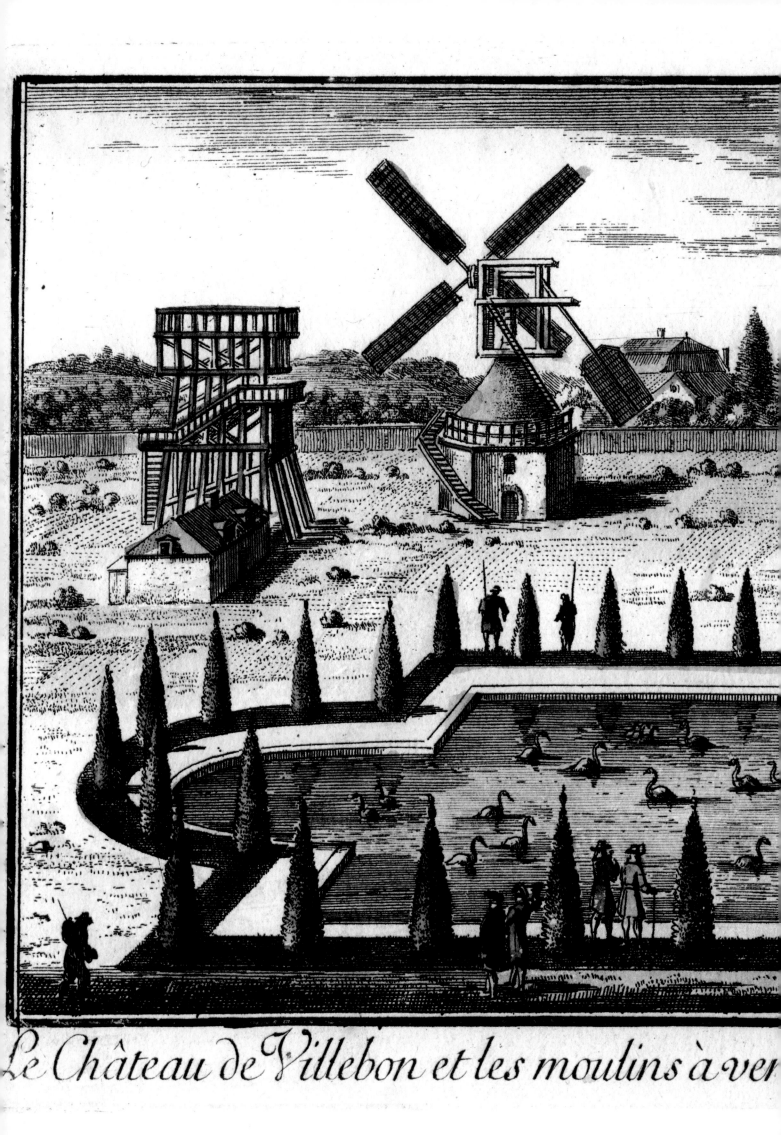

Le Château de Villebon et les moulins à ver

i fournissent les eaux du Chaū de Meudon

HARCOURT

The fortress of Harcourt was the seat of a powerful family founded by a companion of Rollo, the Scandinavian chief who became the first Duke of Normandy following the Treaty of Saint-Clair-sur-Epte in the 10th century. It stands in the Neubourg wheat plain, watered by the Risle.

The Harcourts also owned the castle of Brionne, an old stronghold, but only the keep remains; it is one of the few square keeps to have survived and

stands near one of the great spiritual centers of the medieval world, Le Bec-Hellouin. That district retains many vestiges of past activities: old barns, stables, dovecotes, laundries and mills, which in past times were used by both textile weavers and millers. Behind its imposing walls and wide moats, Harcourt is superbly preserved. An arboretum was established in 1840, only the second in France.

Four hundred species of trees grow there, one of them a cedar of Lebanon which is two hundred and fifty years old.

THE TOWER
OF LE PLANTAY

This massive tower, which is very wide, though not very high, stands beside a dwelling with practically no windows. It is all that remains of the old feudal castle of Le Plantay, burnt, as many of them were (Romans, Rignieux-le-Franc, Sainte-Olive, Chaneins), in 1460 by the troops of the sixth Duke of Bourbon, John II (1426-1488).

In fact the soldiery ravaged the whole of the Dombes area that year. La Dombes, in a region of marshes, lakes and castles, part of the present Ain department, belonged to the Beaujeu family. In 1400 it passed to the Bourbons who raised it to the status of a principality. Later, following the treasonable actions of the Bourbon Constable Charles II, King Francis I would confiscate their lands and make them part of the French kingdom. The commune in which Le Plantay castle was built was called Saint-Didier-de-Renom; it took its present name from the lands of Hugh du Plantay on becoming his property. Antoine de Saint Didier, lord of Le Plantay built the castle on a popye beside a lake.

A *popye* is an artificial mound, there are many of varying height around Europe, particularly common in the Isère and Ain departments. They are remnants of some feudal tradition, funerary monuments perhaps, often now the base for a building. The Le Plantay tower is 60 feet high topped by a parapet walk with machicolations.

ÉPOISSES

Le Grand Condé, victor of Rocroi and unfortunate adversary of Mazarin during the Fronde (17th century revolt of the nobles) owned the castle of Époisses from 1667 to 1672. He loved Burgundy of which he was governor. The big tower in the foreground bears his name: Condé's Tower. They say that as he set out one morning for a day's hunting he said: "What wonderful countryside! What a pity the tower has no balcony so that one could admire it all the time!" When he came back in the evening he was surprised to see a balcony built in one day by his servants.

Whether history or legend, it is rare to see a building like this in Burgundy, containing both rubble and dressed stone. The castle was built in the 11th century in an important strategic position in the Duchy, and was attacked and ruined more than once. Local inhabitants took refuge within its walls in times of danger.

From the 17th century on it was gradually transformed into a residence. In the 18th century revolutionaries knocked down some of its buildings. What remains has frequently been changed, but still bears witness to the wealth and importance of the local owners. For instance the 15th century dovecote has 3000 niches, that number of doves would suggest land holdings of about 7500 acres.

RATILLY

Hidden in the woods and the bracken at the end of a dirt road, Ratilly castle belonged in the 18th century to the Governor of the Duchy of Saint-Fargeau.

La Grande Mademoiselle lived here for a while during her exile for taking part in the Fronde: a revolt of the nobles against royal power. Huguenots sought refuge here during the Wars of Religion, and Jansenists later hid here from the royal police. Behind its fortress-like appearance, the castle is built around a grassy yard.

Today it houses a center for contemporary art, pottery workshops and exhibitions of traditional ceramics. If you visit Guédelon, a few miles away, you get an idea of how they built castles between 1250 and 1350.

In 1997 the master builders' association of Puisaye took on an astonishing task: building a typical 13th century castle, using the tools and methods of the day.

Quarrymen, stone dressers, land clearers, carpenters, smiths all work in a forest clearing, where, as in olden times, they have to find all the materials they need; wood, stone, clay and water.

They work in medieval costume amongst geese, hens and goats, transporting what they need on horse-drawn carts. The charm of the unusual, but also a living history lesson! The builders are backed up by specialists of the medieval period, so as to avoid anything anachronistic. They hope to finish in about 2020.

ANGERS

Louis IX (St Louis) wasn't yet seventeen and his mother, Blanche of Castille, was still regent when, in 1230, he started to build this fortress in Angers.

It was to defend the borders of his kingdom against the ambitions of Henry III of England. The war between France and England would not end until the Treaty of Paris in 1259. The castle of Angers, typical of its day, had seven massive towers in stone of different colors; they were originally 99 feet high, between 36 and 43 feet wide.

There was a wide moat in front of the walls. There were two entrances; one opened to the town the other to the countryside.

This is the one you see in the picture, framed by two towers, in limestone mainly. The oak portcullis was still in place when they started to restore the castle in the last century.

Once the English threat had vanished, King Henry III ordered the castle destroyed. The governor pretended to comply, but in fact strengthened it; he consolidated the towers by reducing their height and using the rubble to create canon emplacements.

BEYNAC

Beynac looks down from a height of nearly five hundred feet over the valley of the Dordogne, near Sarlat and Domme. In the Middle Ages this valley was the border zone between French and English possessions. The rivalry between the lords of Beynac and the lords of Castelnaud, whose castle was on the opposite bank and who favored the English, has remained legendary. The cliffs of this region bristle with seemingly impregnable fortresses. However, the 12th century castle (the one before this one) was taken by Richard the Lion Heart and became an English stronghold. It was later dismantled by Simon de Montfort, during his "crusade" against the Cathars, then rebuilt and captured again by the English during the Hundred Years' War.

The keep and main building date from the 13th and 14th centuries, the Manor house from the 16th. The rampart walk gives a wonderful view of the surrounding countryside. The village huddles at the foot of the cliff, beside the water that reflects the ocher stone so typical of this part of the Périgord.

ANJONY

Anjony is one of the most beautiful stopping places on the high mountain road through the western mountains of Cantal. There are superb views right down into Aurillac. Its high towers sit atop a mountain overlooking the Doire valley, south of Salers.

The citadel is six hundred years old. It was built by a former companion of Joan of Arc and caused a long quarrel between the Anjony family and the Tournemire family whose castle has disappeared. Finally, in the 17th century, the lady who inherited Tournemire married the owner of Anjony.

Its ocher red, basalt walls protect a sumptuous collection of furniture and precious frescoes, some of them show local nobles surrounded by the Nine Valiant Knights. This was a device frequently used from the 14th to the 16th centuries, in all forms of artistic activity, to honor legendary heroes: Alexander the Great, Julius Caesar, Hector, Joshua, David, Judas Maccabeus, King Arthur, Charlemagne, and Godfrey of Bouillon.

108

SULLY-SUR-LOIRE

Between Orléans and Gien, Sully is situated to the south of Germigny-des-Prés. Here Maurice Sully was born into a modest family, yet he became bishop of Paris and masterminded the building of Notre Dame.

In 1602, when Maximilian de Béthune, Henry IV's famous advisor, bought a 14th century castle on the banks of the Loire, the monarch made him Duke of Sully. The Duke made important improvements; in particular he diverted a river

in order to "set" his castle on the water. The keep is flanked by towers and is the oldest part. It still has a totally intact roof structure of chestnut wood.

In the early 18th century the castle was a haven for a young man who had to leave Paris on several occasions, to avoid being flung into the Bastille, because he had annoyed the Regent, Philip of Orléans. The future Voltaire usually made the best of his lot; they built a small theater for him and his wit entertained all the habitués of the salons of Sully, before going on to charm many another.

URRUGNE

Urrugne, former capital of the western Basque province of Labourd, close to the Atlantic and at the entrance of several Pyrenean valleys, is a strategic crossing point into Spain.

In Urrugne in June 1342, Martin de Tartas, the lord of Urrugne, received a letter patent signed at Westminster by the King of England, Edward III, authorizing him to build a castle on the site of the old fortress. He started the work but died in 1343, his brother Arthur finished it. Shortly afterwards the castle fell victim to an unusual occurrence.

In 1463 King Louis XI of France was called on to mediate between the Kings of Castille and Aragon and stayed at Uturbie. He took the lord of the manor, John II, into his service and brought him to Paris. John II soon found himself fighting in Italy in the armies of Charles VIII.

His wife Marie d'Uturbie, fed up of waiting for him to return, or abandoning all hope of seeing him again, remarried and had six children. John II returned and claimed his castle. The Parliament of Bordeaux decided in his favor. His wife, a decidedly fiery woman, set fire to the castle as she left. Now only the keep, a wall and the postern flanked by two towers remain.

A Renaissance-style residence would be built in the 16th century. The castle, a historical monument, is today a hotel.

LA ROCHE-JAGU

Looking at this austere and military building it is difficult to believe it was built by a woman. But it was and its builder was Catherine de Troguindy. She lived from 1340 until 1418 and she inherited the title of Roche-Jagu, which had been created in the 11th century.

A fortress had already been built on top of a cliff overlooking the Trieux estuary in order to protect river traffic and to guard the hinterland. It was destroyed at the end of the 14th century during Wars of Succession in Brittany,

114

which became known as the "War of the two Joans" (Jeanne de Penthièvre against Jeanne de Montfort). The la Roche-Jagu family took the Penthièvre side, but the Montforts won! When peace came in 1365 Catherine de Troguindy had to struggle to get the Duke's permission to rebuild her castle. She succeeded eventually but her most vigorous opponent came from within the family she had earlier supported… the countess of Penthièvre!

The flamboyant gothic castle had a double function; it had a military side, which faced the estuary, and a residential side, which you see in the photo; this is by far the pleasanter side with its round tower and windows overlooking the park.

SAINT-GERMAIN-DE-LIVET

There is surely no other castle like this one. Its two wings are completely different, yet each is typical of the Auge region. The fine building with wooden panels on the right dates from the 15th century; on the left is a building in stone and varnished brick, alternatively white, green and pink. There are elegant towers on either side of the entrance, and a more massive tower to the rear.

The building was put up between 1561 and 1578 with a surrounding moat. Since the Middle Ages the castle of Saint-Germain-de-Livet had been the property of the noble Norman Tournelu family. It was purchased in 1929 by the family of the cabinetmaker Jean-Henri Riesener, and 35 years later given to the town of Lisieux, together with many of the artifacts it contained, including furniture by Jean-Henri Riesener and canvases by his grandson, the painter Léon Riesener.

MARTAINVILLE

Martainville is one of the key stops on the "Normandy-Vexin historical route", going from the outskirts of Rouen to the borders of the Ile de France. It was built in 1485, remodeled at the beginning of the 16th century by a rich merchant from Rouen. Its fine façade of brick set off with stone houses the Museum of Norman Arts and Traditions, with its vast collections of pottery, earthenware, glass work, jewelry, costumes, not forgetting its regional furniture, with superb specimens of Norman wardrobes. Tools and photographs remind us of ancient skills: clog makers, saddlers and weavers.

Two farm buildings surround the central lawn of the castle. The huge octagonal dovecote, built slightly later than the castle and also in brick, contains fifteen hundred niches. This shows how big the estate was as the number of pigeons was proportionate to the size of the land holding. Between castle and dovecote is an enclosed well, a small louvered building roofed with slate, which is typical of the region. In the locality are signs of Normandy's literary heritage. The village of Ry is said to have inspired the setting for Flaubert's Madame Bovary; Delphine Delamare, whose story has similarities with that of Emma, lived there. Flaubert himself said, "Madame Bovary is pure invention"; however this village is full of allusions to the connection.

CHAUMONT

Beautiful Diane de Poitiers must have suffered when her longtime rival, Catherine de Medicis, now the widow of King Henry II, forced her to exchange the elegant arches of Chenonceau for the massive towers of Chaumont!

However Diane de Poitiers left her mark on it and kept it until she died in 1566. It lacks elegance, but it has atmosphere.

Its predecessor on the site had been knocked down by order of Louis XI, because its owner had participated in a revolt of the nobles against royal power. It was rebuilt in two stages. They built the gothic-style northern wing between 1465 and 1475 (it overlooked the Loire and was knocked down in the 18th century to make way for the courtyard overlooking the river), also the west wing, including the enormous "Amboise Tower". Between 1498 and 1510 they built the east wing with the entrance gates and the chapel; they show influences from the Italian Renaissance.

BONAGUIL

It is huge, wonderfully pre-served, has most impressive defenses, yet Bonaguil castle was never once attacked, never experienced the slightest skirmish, was never the scene of any feat of arms. It had no purpose, worse it is the result of a ridiculous local quarrel.

The villain was the local lord, Béranger de Roquefeuil (1441-1530); a bear said his contemporaries, gruff, disagreeable and self-important. He was also lord of a neighboring village and taxed all produce sold there if it weighed over a certain limit. So the villagers saw to it that quantities never reached that limit. Our sly but furious lord sent soldiers to destroy all the weights and measures in the village. Chaos ensued; the villagers threatened Bonaguil.

The lord feared for his life, declared himself persecuted and spent the next thirty years building this formidable fortress in medieval style. It had a barbican, seven drawbridges, a chicane, a blockhouse, canon positions, the thickness of the walls and shape of the keep allowed it to withstand heavy fire… and all this when everywhere else the only castles being built were luxurious country residences.

SULLY

Like its namesake, Sully-sur-Loire, this Burgundy castle owes much of its charm to the mirror of water surrounding it.

In the 13th century, the domain belonged to a Crusader, Gauthier de Sully, before coming into the possession of the Saulx family at the beginning of the 16th century. The Morey family, who built the beautiful classical façade and the massive steps looking out over the water, would later modify it.

In the 18th century an Irish doctor who had taken refuge in France married the widowed lady of Sully. Their grandson was born in Sully in 1808. Count Mac-Mahon had a brilliant military career, earning the rank of Marshal and Duke of Magenta. He would be President of the French Republic from 1873 to 1879.

The "Burgundy Fontainebleau" is near Autun, which owes its name to the Emperor Augustus. The old Roman city, on an important road between Lyon and the northern ports of Gaul, was an important center of Latin culture. It has the largest antique theater ever built in Gaul.

CHAMBORD

"A compendium of human industry" was how the Emperor Charles V described the barely finished Castle of Chambord when King Francis I received him there in 1539.

The building had started twenty years earlier, but had been delayed, because the king had been captured after the Battle of Pavia in 1525. Building later speeded up, but continued, with interruptions, into the reign of Louis XIV. The original plan is attributed to Leonardo da Vinci, particularly the design of the

double spiral staircase in the Guard Room, and which is crowned by a lantern-tower. The works were probably overseen by Dominic de Cortone, nicknamed le Boccador. It is a medieval ground plan, with rich decorations in the Italian style. The central part of the castle is called the "dungeon" and bristles with skylights, towers and chimneys, but there is a garden in front. Kings and queens loved to stay there and hunt in the nearby woods. The dramatist Molière put on Monsieur de Pourceaugnac for the Sun-King in 1669, with music by Lully, and later produced Le Bourgeois Gentilhomme. This "magical" castle, according to the poet Alfred de Vigny, is the biggest of the Loire Valley Castles and its white outline roofed with slates is a symbol of the Renaissance.

CHENONCEAU

This Renaissance masterpiece, built over the water, stands on the foundations of an old mill. They started building it in 1513, a few short years before Chambord or Azay-le-Rideau. Here, as at Azay, the works were overseen by a woman, Catherine Briçonnet, while her husband, Thomas Bohier, the Director General of Finance for Normandy, was fighting in the Italian wars.

The estate was then ceded to Constable Montmorency, who took possession of it in the name of the crown, before Henry II gave it as a gift to his favorite, Diane de Poitiers. She loved it and strongly influenced its development: notably by bridging the river Cher and laying out superb gardens. Twelve years later, when the king died, she was soon evicted by his widow Catherine de Medicis, who remodeled both buildings and gardens with the help of Bernard Palissy. In 1577, she opened the two-storied gallery built on the bridge, with a sumptuous feast in honor of Henry III. In the 18th century Chenonceau would be the scene of other lavish receptions. Madame Dupin, its new owner, entrusted Jean-Jacques Rousseau with the education of her son and entertained the great thinkers of the age: Voltaire, Montesquieu, Buffon, and Marivaux.

Chenonceau welcomes more visitors than any other castle in France.

128

SACHÉ

"At Saché I'm happy and free, like a monk in his monastery. The sky is so pure, the oaks so beautiful, the calm so complete."

Honoré de Balzac discovered Saché when, in 1823, friends of his parents, the Margonne family (Mr. de Margonne was his mother's lover), bought the castle which was in fact a charming 16th and 17th century manor house. He would spend long periods there from 1823 to 1837. In those days it only took 23 hours to get by coach from Paris to Tours, and then there would only be another 12 miles to travel; when he was broke, Balzac did it on foot!

The castle was built, as was often the case, on the foundations of a medieval fortress; a tower and the moat still stood. The writer lived in a cell rather than in a room: with just a bed and a desk! It was here that he wrote *Old Goriot* and *The Lily in the Valley*.

Balzac fans are delighted to find how comparable are the places described in the novels and the places he really lived in. Today Saché castle is a museum.

130

VALENÇAY

Valençay is quite a bit away from other "Loire Valley Castles", in reality it is closer to the Cher to the south of the Sologne region. It was built in the 16th and 17th centuries, in an elegant classical style, yet still with Renaissance hints. "La Grande Mademoiselle" as the Duchess of Montpensier was known, was overwhelmed: "I thought I was coming to an enchanted castle. It is the most beautiful and most magnificent residence in the world."

It was briefly the property of John Law, who is as well known for his financial abilities as for the bankruptcy that sent him suddenly into exile in 1720. Talleyrand bought the property in 1803. Then in his fifties, he was half way through his long and slippery career. Napoleon I would name him Grand Chamberlain the following year, before disgracing him in 1809. In the meantime the Emperor had placed his eldest brother Joseph on the throne of Spain and installed the deposed king here. A sumptuous prison, but a prison none the less. Ferdinand VII remained here seven years, until his jailor abdicated.

TANLAY

The castle of Tanlay combines Renaissance elegance with the solidity of Burgundy. Beneath its steep slate roofs you see evidence of successive stages of construction, part of it being the "little castle", from the time of Louis XIII.

The two pyramids on either side of the bridge leading to the main courtyard were modified in the 17th century to make the Great Gallery and decorated in trompe-l'oeil.

134

The so-called "League" tower reminds us that Protestant leaders often met at Tanlay. The Prince of Condé, one of their leaders, owned the castle at Noyers a little to the south and the Coligny family, who were also leading Calvinists, owned Tanlay during the Wars of Religion. The painted ceiling of the top floor represents many members of the family as mythological figures. The castle moat is fed by a long canal crossing the grounds. Tanlay is built near the River Armançon, between Tonnerre, famous for its Fosse Dionne spring water, and the castle of Ancy-le-Franc, another Renaissance masterpiece.

BUSSY-RABUTIN

This elegant castle stands close to the Abbey of Fontenay, but reminds us of a character who was anything but monk-like! The solid towers recall the original fortress, three façades have a Renaissance look, but the fourth was redeveloped in the reign of Louis XIV by its most famous owner, Roger de Rabutin, Count of Bussy.

This soldier-writer redecorated the interior to suit his own taste. We find great soldiers and well-known courtesans, each given a motto composed by himself. They are both witty and impertinent. The king is described as "both the delight and the terror of the human race".

The king was not amused and exiled the Count to his lands in Burgundy. But our incorrigible libertine just sat down to write his *Love History of the Gauls*, in which he gave a gleefully malicious account of court life. His exile was consequently interrupted by residence in the Bastille. His bedroom has a gallery with portraits of women; amongst them his famous cousin, Madame de Sévigné: "the loveliest girl in France" according to him.

The Marquise de Sévigné wrote some fifteen hundred letters, full of confidences, pen portraits, the gossip and happenings of the day. They are now much better known than the writings of the Count who, in his day, was a member of the French Academy.

136

CLOS VOUGEOT

Known worldwide, because in the heart of the best Burgundy vineyards, the Clos Vougeot castle is, paradoxically, an offshoot product of the Abbey of Cîteaux. The Cistercian tradition was established in 1098 by a handful of monks who, wishing to break with the luxurious lifestyle of the Abbey of Cluny, had left their abbey at Molesme, a short distance away and had built, between Dijon and Beaune, a new (wooden) abbey, where they resolved to follow the Rule of St Benedict in a manner that can be summed up in two words: poverty and prayer. Now, unlike choir monks who could not leave the abbey, the lay brothers could reside outside the walls in order to work the lands given by local lords or indeed

138

bought by the abbey. Naturally these lands were planted with vines and produced excellent wine. Between 1116 and 1160 the lay brothers enclosed the vineyard, the wall still stands, and built the necessary buildings and a cellar. Added to and improved over the centuries, they are a remarkable set of buildings.

The building housing the vats has four galleries, one hundred feet by thirty, around a central tower with four gigantic presses with an oak capstan: the cellar, whose roof is supported by eight beautiful stone pillars, can hold two thousand casks of wine. In 1551 the 43rd abbot of Cîteaux, Dom Jean Loisier, added to these working buildings, by constructing a luxurious dwelling.

Clos Vougeot is presently the biggest first class vineyard on the Côte de Nuits. It is over one hundred and twenty-six acres in size and worked by eighty proprietors.

BLÉRANCOURT

A revolution laid it low; a war revived it. Such is the tragic, but magnificent destiny of Blérancourt castle in the Aisne region. Solomon de Brosse built it between 1612 and 1619 at the request of Bernard Potier de Gesvres, a friend of Henry IV and Queen Margot; this extraordinary man protected artists and scholars and was an important landowner in Picardy.

The castle is a wonderful example of classical architecture. But it was sacked at the Revolution, sold and due to be dismantled. Only two wings remained and no doubt these two survivors would also have disintegrated were it not for the generosity of the daughter of the American banker, John Pierpoint Morgan. Her aim was not to save the castle, but civilian victims of the First World War. In 1917 Ann Morgan was allowed to house war refugees in Blérancourt. When peace returned, she gathered memorabilia of the American involvement in the war and turned the building into a moving "museum of Franco-American cooperation".

BARBENTANE

In this wonderful corner of the foothills of the Alps they call it the "Little Trianon in the sun".

Looking at its classical façade, you would think you were in the Île-de-France. In the reign of Louis XIV architects sought elegance, harmony, balance. The builder Paul-François de Barbentane faithfully followed the plans drawn up

by his father in 1654. But the astonishing contrast is between the façade, which is as it was built in 1674, and the interior that was totally renewed a hundred years later, by the builder's grandson, in the luxurious style of 18th century Italian palaces.

Louis XV had sent Joseph Pierre Balthazar de Brabentane as ambassador to the Duke of Tuscany in 1768. He returned determined to reproduce the Florentine decorative art he had admired so much while abroad.

VAUX-LE-VICOMTE

Vaux-le-Vicomte reminds us of the motto that its builder had chosen for himself: "How high shall I not rise?" Fouquet, a protégé of Mazarin, was Superintendent General of Finances in the reign of Louis XIV.

Some of the most brilliant artists of the day cooperated to build his castle: Le Vau, Le Brun, Le Nôtre. In 1661, with the work barely complete, he threw a lavish party at which Molière produced his play, *Les Fâcheux*,

in the gardens. "Everything at Vaux competed to please the king, music, water, chandeliers and stars", wrote Jean de La Fontaine.

But the King, who had just that year begun his personal rule, was not amused. The fabulously wealthy Finance Superintendent was arrested a few days after the dazzling reception.

The King however approved of his taste and would later employ those who had created Vaux to transform Versailles. Fouquet's castle remains a perfect example of French classical style.

VERSAILLES

This handsome statue by Jean-Baptiste Tuby dates from the late 17th century and represents the river Rhône. It is part of the series of eight symbols of France's rivers ornamenting the "Parterre d'Eau", the two rectangular pools, called North and South, that were created in 1684-85 in front of the palace's terrace.

In the photo we glimpse the terrace, but the most striking feature is the "new" castle designed by the architect Le Vau and built of stone and marble in 1668-70. It surrounds Louis XIII's "old" castle and provided the much larger living space called for by Louis XIV. Versailles is the most beautiful castle in France and it was here that Louis XIV established the most elegant court in Europe.

CHANTILLY

The name Chantilly alone is enough to conjure up the greatest families of France's nobility: Montmorency, Condé, Bourbon, Aumale and Orléans, all of whom contributed to the nation's history, sometimes with enormous verve and sometimes in the register of tragedy. Anne de Montmorency (1493-1567) was Constable of France and fought beside François I at Marignan. His grandson Henri II de Montmorency (1595-1632) was beheaded on the orders of Louis XIII for leading the Languedoc rising. At Chantilly the magnificent warrior, rebellious

adventurer and sometime traitor Louis II de Bourbon-Condé, known as the Great Condé (1621-1686), brought together all Paris' leading artists, writers and philosophers, among them La Fontaine, Molière, La Bruyère, Bossuet and Mesdames de Lafayette and de Sévigné. Louis-Joseph, Prince de Condé (1736-1818), left France on 17 July 1789 and organized the counter-Revolutionary "emigrant army". His son, the duke of Enghien (1772-1804), was shot on the orders of Napoleon. Henri d'Orléans, duke of Aumale (1822-1897) and son of King Louis-Philippe, rebuilt the castle – destroyed during the Revolution – lost his wife and two children, and collected works of art that he bequeathed to the Institut de France, with the castle, in 1884.

FONTAINEBLEAU

Begun in 1527 after the Italian campaigns, Fontainebleau is usually referred to as "the château of François I". But it has also been the home of thirty-four other sovereigns, almost all of whom, in one way or another, renovations, modifications or additions, made their own contributions to this splendid site down the centuries. In the Cour du Cheval-Blanc, known since Napoleon's time as the Cour des Adieux, the famous Horseshoe Staircase dates from the 17th century;

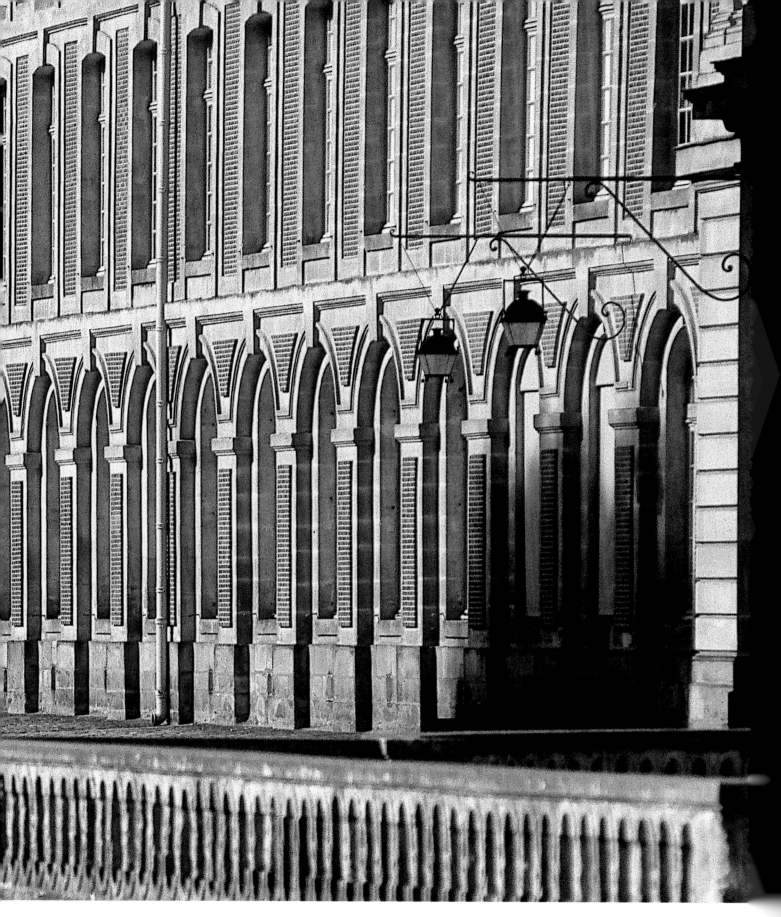

the Porte Dauphine, giving onto the Cour Ovale, is from the time of Louis XIII; the Chinese Museum was created by Empress Eugénie; the Chapelle de la Trinité was decorated by Henri IV; the interior decoration is a wonderful mix of all styles; and Louis XIV planted hundreds of trees in the grounds and had a small pavilion built in the middle of the Etang des Carpes. This is the pavilion shown in the photo above: note the very 18th-century look of the Louis XV wing. It was designed by Jacques Ange Gabriel, chief royal architect, also the guiding spirit behind the Petit Trianon in Versailles and Place de la Concorde in Paris.

HAROUÉ

Voltaire often lived in Lunéville towards the end of the 1740s, but made frequent stays at Haroué castle to which he had a permanent invitation; he was the most prestigious and wittiest guest you could imagine.

Voltaire's real name was François Marie d'Arouet; Haroué and Arouet: same sound, different spelling! The philosopher often spoke of "his" castle

at Haroué. It had in fact been built between 1720 and 1732 for the Viceroy of Tuscany and Constable of Lorraine, Marc Beauvau de Craon. The architect Germain Boffrand had built on the foundations of a Renaissance stronghold maintaining the original ground plan of 4 towers, but he added 12 turrets, 52 chimneys and 365 windows: perhaps because it was the century of the Enlightenment, or because there are 365 days in the year.

TOWNS AND CITIES

Cities were built in the countryside, said one humorist. But they have now more or less taken over the countryside, spreading out their suburbs and their industrial parks, creating mile after mile of compact networks of roads. But for the historian the difference between city and village has less to do with the amount of space taken as with the occupations of the citizens. The village was essentially agricultural, the city, which was once the place of exchange, commerce and a center of civil and religious administration, is now devoted to the services sector.

Cities built on a river, supplying it with water and facilitating trade, developed quickly: Paris, Orléans, Lyon, Toulouse, Amiens, Rennes and Strasbourg amongst others. Likewise ports trading in spices, which were worth a king's ransom in the Middle Ages. When open to the ocean and the New World, they flourished. Marseille, a Mediterranean port, prospered because of its links with the east; other cities developed inland where two major trade routes crossed; others grew up around an important religious center. Today their city centers bear eloquent witness to the societies that, over the centuries, fashioned them.

THE ROMAN CITIES OF GAUL

The earliest signs we still possess are those from the Roman cities of Gaul. Most of our modern regional capitals started in this way. On the other hand a number of Gaulish cities declined under the Romans. Caesar's armies, for example, sacked Avaricum, " the biggest and best fortified city of the Biturges, situated in a very fertile region", to quote Caesar himself. Modern Bourges, capital of Aquitaine from the 1st to the 4th centuries, would not prosper again until the Middle Ages, under Jean de Berry, the famous sponsor of the lavishly decorated book of religious services called Les Très Riches Heures du Duc de Berry and made by the Limbourg brothers. Jacques Coeur, financier and counselor to Charles VII, took up the city's cause; he established his principal residence there.

The names of those ancient Gaulish tribes still echo in the names of modern cities. The Remi gave their name to Reims, the Ruteni to the inhabitants of Rodez, the Tolsati lived in Toulouse, the Santoni in Saintonges and Saintes, the Veneti at Vannes, the Senones at Sens. Later Clovis would choose Lutetia as his capital. This little town was renamed Paris in the 4th century after the Parisii, a tribe who had lived on the l'Île de la Cité before the Romans came.

Lyon, which was founded by the Romans, gets its name from Lugdunum, in the Celtic language this is the "Fortress of Lugh" (the sun god). Aix-en-Provence, on the other hand, is the old Aquae Sextiae, the "waters of Sextius". This consul destroyed the hill fort of the Salieni at Entremont to build below it, near the springs, the city which would become the capital of the Provincia Romana. Marseille had asked the Romans to intervene. This city of the Phoceans was then an ally of Rome in seeking to limit Carthaginian power in the Mediterranean.

In addition to houses and administrative centers, the Roman cities of Gaul were centers of trade and skilled craftsmen; one finds market places, triumphal arches, temples, fountains, and leisure centers: baths, arenas, theaters and walkways. These elements would remain permanent features of the city, with only modest changes. The Romans have put their stamp on Arles, Orange, Vaison, Vienne and Nîmes. Roman remains are naturally more numerous in the south, which was the heart of the Roman conquest before the Gallic War ended in 51 BC. However Autun, on the main road between Lyon and the northern ports of Gaul, has the biggest ancient theater built in Gaul. The network of the main roads, allowing both trade and troop movements from one end of the territory to the other, is another inheritance from Roman times.

MEDIEVAL CITIES

After the fall of the Roman Empire, the cities and the roads between them were often allowed to decay. Invasion followed invasion; towns were pillaged and sacked. A new form of the nomadic lifestyle returned. People took shelter in the forests and in castles and monasteries. The cultivated lands of the monasteries were a precious resource. These were often built on the foundations of the old Roman buildings or using their stones. Cities were born, or reborn, under their protection: Blois and Pau were built around a fortress, Vézelay and Arras around a religious foundation.

For centuries they remained defensive in character. They had to be defended against invasions (Vandals, Visigoths, Huns, Vikings…), but also against the rivalries that were part and parcel of the tangle of feudal loyalties of the Middle Ages. This continued right up to the battles and sieges of the Hundred Years' War.

In the Middle Ages, traders and craftsmen organized themselves into guilds, while bishops developed their power. The seeds of later conflicts between civil and religious authorities were already being sown. Each side had its geographical area, like Rodez with its two great squares: Cathedral Square and Market Square. Soon some of the nobility would abandon their castles, hemmed in by the city, for residences built outside the walls. Bishops and "bourgeois" will soon start struggling for power. The businessmen will set up their operations around the town and then these suburbs will be taken into the city. Street names often remind us how the different trades necessary for community life had their own areas: des Orfèvres (Goldsmiths), des Tanneurs (tanners), de la Coutellerie (cutlers), des Merciers (mercers, haberdashers or notions dealers)…

Cities with great markets or fairs prospered, like Troyes and Provins in Champagne; they still contain marvelous medieval houses. Others benefited from being the seat of a powerful lord. Dijon was transformed in the 14th century under the Dukes of Burgundy. Philip the Bold, having married Marguerite of Flanders, reigned over a territory where exceptional artistic gifts flourished, particularly in his capital, but also at Arras and Lille. These two northern cities, famous for their cloth weavers and tapestry makers still preserve their squares, belfries and exchanges so typical of Flemish cities. Toulouse also, ruled by its Counts and capitouls (local magistrates), flourished at this time.

Cities were becoming cultural centers, students were pouring in. The Sorbonne was one of the first universities, founded in 1257, while Montpellier, already graced by schools of Medicine and Law, founded its university in 1289, some fifteen years earlier than that of Orléans. In the 14th century people no longer relied on church bells to tell the time: in 1370 Charles V had public clocks installed in Paris, the earliest being that in the Courts of Justice.

FROM THE RENAISSANCE TO THE ENLIGHTENMENT

When Renaissance society looked back to the Ancient world for inspiration it discovered a text that would have a profound effect on all builders: De Architectura by Vitruvius, a contemporary of Julius Caesar. He laid down three architectural principles: solidity, convenience and beauty.

The defensive look was out! Builders now wanted to emphasize beauty; the invention of artillery and the possibility of bombardment had made defensive architecture pointless. In the cities that princes, ministers and high financiers were modernizing and beautifying, anything that suggested the countryside would soon disappear. The pigs that cleaned the streets, the hens in yards behind the houses, the kitchen gardens for vegetables no longer had a place.

Many cities were transformed by the discovery of the New World, particularly the ports, whose activity increased tenfold. In Bordeaux and Nantes, bankers, ship owners and businessmen all built sumptuous houses. These new houses, like the new château-manor houses then being built would create new needs and earn new fortunes. Rouen prospered because of its textiles and earthenware. The center of Lyon was filled with new prosperous town houses, paid for by the silk industry. The area of Strasbourg known as la Petite France was being built, like la Petite Venise in Colmar; they were exceptional sets of buildings, houses with wooden panels, corbelled windows and balconies, mostly built beside the canal for the Renaissance tanners of the city. In the center of Clermont-Ferrand look for beautiful houses built for merchants, the Apothecary's House, or for city officers: l'Hôtel de Fontfreyde. Toulouse got suddenly rich from a short-lived but enormous demand for pastel, and many superb town houses were built there.

At the same time, city dwellers were experiencing innovations that would influence the lives of all citizens of the kingdom and impose a degree of uniformity unknown up to then. In 1539 the decree of Villers-Cotterêts would set up the public registry system, establish the civil status of every citizen and lay down French as the official language for all legal and administrative documents.

The first signs of what we now call public transport would appear in 1576; it linked Paris, Rouen, Beauvais, Amiens, Troyes and Orléans. Up to then the postal system had been reserved exclusively for royal letters, it now became a public service.

About 1610 building started on the Île St Louis in Paris, a little after the opening of the Place Royale, now Place des Vosges. Other squares designed to be the backdrop for a statue of the sovereign would be built during the reigns of Louis XIV and Louis XV: Place Bellecour in Lyon and Place Stanislas in Nancy. Large gardens were now being developed in cities, together with long walks, and paved thoroughfares where one could display one's coach and pair.

THE CHANGES BROUGHT BY INDUSTRIALIZATION

Improving traffic flow became important as industrialization developed. The notion of the "ideal" industrial city was born just before the Revolution: Claude-Nicholas Ledoux planned the royal Salt works at Arc-et-Senans so as to combine, in a bright, open location, both working space and living space for all involved: from the humblest workers right up to the manager.

This utopian scheme, like the later proposals of Charles Fourier, which also sought to improve living conditions, had few backers. An exception is the familistère built by Jean-Baptiste Godin at Guise and which he bequeathed to his staff. In nineteenth century Mulhouse, industrialists designed a housing estate where each family had a house with a garden. The "Industrial Society" was set up to fulfill an educative function, by founding museums and schools. But more frequently cities absorbed the workers the new industries needed to run them, in a totally haphazard fashion. A new population of workers was arriving in the cities and towns to supply the huge new factories. They piled into old, chaotic and unsanitary buildings where epidemics frequently broke out: cholera in Paris for example in the first half of the 19th century. We are now in the city of Balzac and Zola, where misery and magnificence rub shoulders. This situation is not new, but is emphasized by the increasing number of places where the well heeled gathered: cafés, restaurants, operas, theaters, and the latest fashion: department stores, Bon Marché in Paris being the world's first. The poor were progressively pushed out to the margins; the city centers were increasingly reserved for businesses and those who ran them.

The tightly packed city centers were cleared out to build wide squares and broad avenues. Railway stations were now being built using cast-iron architecture. Eiffel in particular designed the frame of Bon-Marché before going on to build the tower that would become the symbol of Paris. New shopping areas would often use such cast-iron frames: covered arcades like the famous Passage Pommeraye in Nantes. But the great openings made by Baron Haussmann, creating long straight boulevards, cutting through old buildings right up to Notre Dame, have, according to himself, two aims which have nothing to do with hygiene: "to make the old buildings stand out, thus making them more pleasing to the eye and to make the city more easy to protect in case of riot".

DURING THE SECOND EMPIRE

The Second Empire saw the start of another craze that would snowball in time: going to the seaside. "Extremely stylish villas" to use Proust's phrase, were built in fishing villages. Their developers turned them into seaside resorts, with a "British" air; all this delighted the aristocrats who had fled to England during the 1830 and 1848 revolutions. From 1850 on, hotels and villas sprouted up around the casino in Trouville. The board walkway became the fashionable place to meet and to be seen; the same must be said for its neighbor Deauville, a town put on the fashion map by the Emperor's half brother the Duke of Morny. In the 1850s at Le Touquet, they planted a forest of pine and birch; and nestling amongst them, luxurious houses.

The Riviera was equally successful: Cannes had La Croisette, Nice had the Promenade des Anglais and later Menton would develop the Promenade du Soleil.

THE TWENTIETH CENTURY

The look of many cities would be affected by the two twentieth century World Wars. Huge reconstruction programs would be needed to restore the wreckage: Le Havre, totally destroyed in 1944, is a good example. Auguste Perret would oversee rebuilding work after the war. He was the first architect to put up a building in reinforced concrete in Paris (1903); he then went on to build the Champs Élysées Theater. This was the style he would use for Le Havre Town Hall, which overlooks a huge open space, prolonged by Avenue Foch.

At a time when housing was in short supply, and people were leaving the countryside at an increasing rate, there was a huge building program on the outskirts of cities. Architects and town planners were constantly on the look out for new styles of social housing and they wanted it to be a complete break with the traditions of the past. Of these, Le Corbusier is no doubt the best known. In 1922 he presented his "plan for a city of three million inhabitants". He thought of the home as a "machine for living in", he built The Radiant City (la Cité Radieuse) on the outskirts of Marseille; it would be renamed the "Barmy House" (la maison du Fada), by those not impressed by his utopian dream. In Paris he wanted to knock down the Marais, whose elegant houses and old-fashioned courtyards had been turned into workshops and warehouses; his plan was to cover it with tower blocks: happily this plan was abandoned.

Unlike the preceding century, when Viollet-le-Duc restored buildings by depending largely on personal inspiration, the 20th century has tried to conserve our architectural heritage in as authentic a fashion as possible. This task is difficult to reconcile with modern styles of living, and above all, with that new urban phenomenon: traffic! Following a period when the motorcar was king, they are now trying to recreate pedestrian areas in old streets, where one can better appreciate and enjoy all the signs of the past. It is quite a feat to get the Pompidou Center at Beaubourg and the St Merri church, the Bastille Opera House and the paved courtyards of the Faubourg St Antoine, Sophia-Antipolis and the old streets of Antibes, to sit comfortably side by side. This audacious plan has often paid off. It at least has the merit of not freezing a streetscape into museum format; that was never what streets were about. Streets are for living in and "every city is a state of mind, and when we live there for a while, that state of mind seeps into us, invading us rather as we absorb the air we breathe." (Georges Rodenbach)

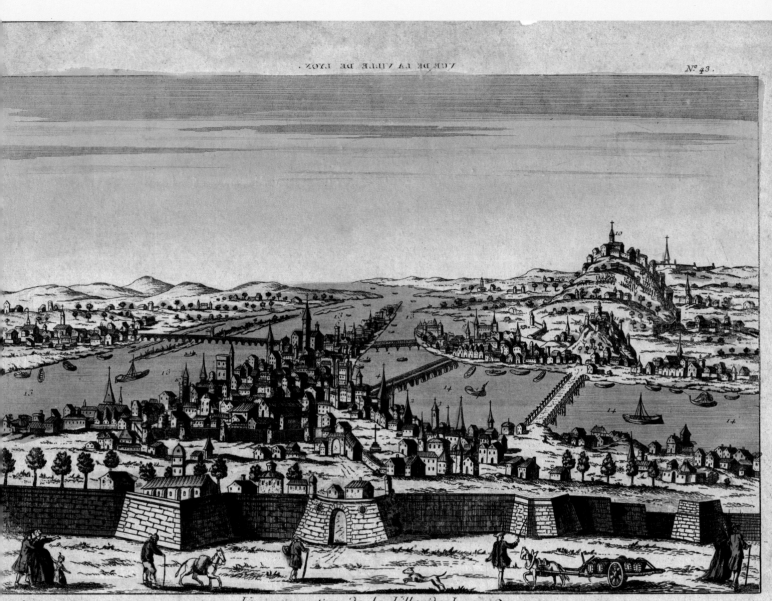

Vue perspective de la Ville de Lyon

A Paris chez Jacques Chereau rue St Jacques au dessus de la Fontaine St Severin. Nᵒ 257.

St Sebastien. 3. les Carmelites. 5. St Nizier. 7. St Antoine 9. St Just. 11. Pierre Cise. 13. le Rosne Riviere. 15. la Guilletiere.
les Chartreux. 4. les Augustins. 6. les Celestins. 8. Ainée Abbaye. 10. Forviere. 12. St Jean Cathedrale. 14. la Saone Riviere. 16. les Cordelliers.

BERGUES
THE FORTRESS

The town of Bergues owes its name to the green hill (Groenberg in Flemish) on which it is built.

About 700 AD, St Winoc, a Breton monk, chose this hill for his hermitage and set about converting Flanders. Gradually a town grew up around the abbey, which was many times captured and freed, ruined and rebuilt; Flanders was for many centuries border territory.

Bergues finally became French in 1668 at the Treaty of Aix-la-Chapelle. Vauban was then ordered to fortify it. It had been a stronghold in the Middle Ages, The Bierne Tower, in the photo, dates from that period. The square castle had two round towers with great firepower and two smaller towers behind.

In the 16th century the Spanish rebuilt the town and the defenses. But it was Louis XIV's architect who gave it such thick walls, adapted to the warfare of the day and skillfully arranged. Unusually for him there was water in the moat; it was not just a dry ditch.

ROUEN
THE GREAT CLOCK

There had been a tower there originally. But in 1356 the merchants who administered the town of Rouen, rose up against the king who was crushing them with taxes. The Harelle Revolt, as it was called, was opposed with arms and severely repressed: Charles VI abolished the corporation and razed the tower where it held its meetings. Thirty years later the new town authority, headed by a bailiff, built the clock tower in its place. Later again, in 1527, an arch was built over the street to join belfry and Town Hall.

It is a beautiful Renaissance building with the faces of a new and superb clock on the sides. A single hand, with a tiny sheep at the tip, points to the hours. Above the clock face, a ball turns in its casing; it is the moon, one of its sides is black the other silver; it turns twice in 59 days: twelve lunar months.

Beneath the clock face, a little rectangular screen shows the planets, one for each day of the week: Diana for Monday, Mars for Tuesday (mardi), Mercury for Wednesday (mercredi), Jupiter for Thursday (jeudi), Venus for Friday (vendredi), Saturn for Saturday and Apollo for Sunday. The belfry clock still works, flanked by two bells: one sounds the curfew every evening at nine o'clock, it has now been doing this for 550 years to keep the memory of the Hundred Years' War alive.

ALBI
THE ENGELBERT HOUSE

Albi was a simple fortified village in the 7th century; it gradually grew into a town, then a city. First the bridge was built across the Tarn in 1040, then it became famous for trading in cloth, corn and pastel.

The Renaissance buildings all over the city reveal how rich the city traders became in the 16th and 17th centuries

The Engelbert house is striking because its structure is medieval, its decoration Renaissance.

As in earlier buildings, the ground floor is open to the street and was used as a shop; the corbeled upper stories hang out over the street. But gothic features, gables (triangular pediments), pinnacles and accolades have all disappeared to be replaced by classical decoration: pilasters, cartouches, composite capitals and pediments.

165

BEAUNE
THE HÔTEL-DIEU

Contemplating the munificence of the Hôtel-Dieu in Beaune, it is difficult to imagine that it was a hospital up until 1971. Built in the 15th century by Chancellor Nicholas Rolin, an advisor to the Dukes of Burgundy; he conducted many negotiations for them during the struggles between Armagnacs and Burgundians and amassed colossal wealth. With the support of his wife, Guigone de Salins, Rolin devoted part of his wealth to founding this hospice at the end of the Hundred Years' War. Some people have interpreted the gesture as the need to ease an over-burdened conscience.

The Hôtel-Dieu was sometimes seen as the eighth wonder of the world and is a masterpiece of flamboyant gothic art in Burgundy. It reflects the astonishing power of Duke Philip the Good. In the central courtyard, steep roofs covered with varnished tiles, and pierced with dormer windows topped by weather vanes, display their patterns of brown, red and ocher. This splendid roof has become a symbol for the city.

The wards have been, to a large extent, furnished as they originally were. The biggest, opening onto a chapel, is covered by a magnificent polychrome wooden ceiling. In the kitchen a 17th century wooden machine turns the spit in an enormous fireplace, and in the pharmacy you may see a collection of pewter and earthenware pots. When the Hôtel-Dieu was converted to a museum, one room was especially adapted to house the many-paneled painting of the Last Judgment. This is Van der Weyden's masterpiece. He was the official painter of the city of Brussels and was commissioned by Nicholas Rolin to decorate the chapel of the main ward. The painting remained there until the Revolution.

MARSEILLE
THE OLD CHARITY HOSPITAL

It was Marseille's "poor asylum". And proved that functional architecture can be beautiful. In 1640 a royal edict forced city authorities to remove beggars from public roads. Three years later Marseille opened this building to house them. You could not imagine a simpler plan: four blocks around a central courtyard: with three stories of galleries overlooking it.

The photo is of the chapel in the middle of the courtyard. It was built by local architect Pierre Puget and is crowned by a baroque oval dome. It housed the orphans and vagabonds of Marseille for over a century. In the 18th and 19th centuries it housed orphans and old people only (were there really no more vagabonds?). In the 20th century the buildings were abandoned (no more orphans or old people either?). It was eventually rescued from ruin by Le Corbusier (amongst others) and is today an active cultural center. FOLLOWING PAGES

AVIGNON
THE PALACE
OF THE POPES

In 1309, Pope Clement V chose to live in the Dominican convent in Avignon, rather than in Italy, which was then suffering from political instability. The former bishop of the city succeeded him in 1316, taking the name of John XXII. He adapted the bishop's palace, near the cathedral, but Benedict XII, elected in 1334, knocked it down and built instead a veritable citadel bristling with powerful towers. Today it is called "The Old Palace". Eight years later, Clement VI added "The New Palace", which was constructed by Jean de Louvres and decorated by an artist from Viterbo called Matteo Giovannetti.

He painted the works in the chapels dedicated to St John and to St Martial and in the main audience hall. This set of buildings was one of the biggest residences of its day, concealing sumptuous apartments behind an austere exterior. Popes, each making his own changes, would live here until 1377, when Gregory XI brought the papacy back to Rome.

Then the Great Schism divided Christianity, the cardinals refused to recognize the authority of Urban VI and elected an "antipope", Clement VII, who also resided at Avignon, as did his successor Benedict XIII. Since 1947 the main yard of the palace has been the setting for the prestigious Theater Festival created by Jean Vilar, it has now largely outgrown its original location.

PARIS
THE PONT NEUF

This might be the oldest of all the bridges of Paris, but it has kept the "New Bridge" nickname it was given when it was built in 1578-1604.

Not only was it the newest bridge at the time, it was also the most innovative, being the first not to be lined with houses and shops in the manner of the Ponte Vecchio in Florence.

The top of each pile opens out in a half-moon shape, leaving room for street entertainers to ply their trade. This was, too, the first thoroughfare in the capital with footpaths for pedestrians.

Along its entire length are grimacing figures sculpted in stone, said to be caricatures of all the advisers, ministers and friends of the king who were opposed to the building of the bridge: instead of punishment, Henri IV opted for ridicule…

LILLE
THE OLD STOCK EXCHANGE

Lille, the principal city of the County of Flanders, owed its prosperity to trade. Situated at a major crossroads within the territory of the dynamic dukes of Burgundy, Lille nonetheless had to cope with the competition of the Dutch in the course of an ongoing struggle to maintain and increase its wealth. Thus the building of the old Stock Exchange by the city architect

Julien Destrée in 1652-53 was personally financed by the local merchants: they were keen to prevent Antwerp from gaining a monopoly and needed a place were they could do business discreetly.

This explains the architecture of the building: a square courtyard formed by twenty-four identical houses whose ground floor acted as a foundation and whose two upper floors of stone and brick were richly ornamented.

LA ROCHELLE
THE CITY HALL

"The most beautiful building in the city", say the inhabitants. They are right to be proud of it, for it is indeed superb architecture: its oldest stones go back to the end of the 15th century. Before it was built the aldermen met, on this site, in a set of five houses, about which only one thing is known: a fire reduced them to ashes.

Rebuilding started in 1486 at the same time as the city wall, which still stands, with its towers, its external stairway, its lantern. The magnificent Renaissance gallery you see here dates from the early years of the 17th century. It is part of the main building, put up by master mason Favreau between 1605 and 1606; the following year the Aldermen's building was started behind this main building, along the rue des Gentils-hommes.

Every century has brought changes to this prestigious City Hall, and the 19th century more than any other when they rebuilt the main building, the external stairway, lengthened the gallery with a ninth bay, added a belfry to the top of the north tower, adding a façade and a further building, but hardly destroying anything (with the exception of the external stairway) and always mindful of the original.

It is a classified and protected monument of course, which is visited not only by the citizens of La Rochelle, but also by thousands of tourists!

NANCY
PLACE STANISLAS

The gates of Place Stanislas demonstrate the grace that certain 18th century artists could attain. Stanislas Leszczynski, former king of Poland and father-in-law to Louis XV, rebuilt the center of Nancy in the 18th century. He had received the Duchy of Lorraine for his lifetime and encouraged artists and scientists to work both there and in Lunéville.

To build this square, then called "Place Royale", he called on the architect Emmanuel Héré de Corny and on the wrought iron worker Jean Lamour who decorated the wrought iron railings with subtle designs in gold.

Nancy would later be one of the places where Art Nouveau would shine thanks to Emile Gallé, Louis Majorelle, Eugene Vallin and the Daum brothers, amongst others.

178

BORDEAUX
STOCK EXCHANGE SQUARE

Place de la Bourse is evidence of the 18th century prosperity of Bordeaux, and of the troubles that followed. It had many names: Royal Square, Liberty Square, Imperial Square, Royal Square again, finally Stock Exchange Square.

There was once an equestrian statue of Louis XV which was melted down, of Napoleon III (thrown into the river), today of the three Graces.

Laid out by Jacques Gabriel and his son (they built the Little Trianon in Versailles) in the reign of Louis XV, it is surrounded by three baroque buildings; the fourth side faces the river. Once the neglected site of ugly sheds and chaotic traffic, it has recovered its ancient splendor.

CASTRES

HOUSES OVERLOOKING THE AGOUT

The town grew up after 647 around a Benedictine Abbey. The name (from the Latin castrum) reminds us that Roman armies had once occupied the site. It was famous in the 16th century when Henry IV made it the seat of one of the five Chambers of the Edict of the Kingdom. The function of these chambers was to hear cases involving Protestants.

This was when the beautiful town houses overlooking the river Agout were built. They are the pride and joy of Castres. The wool and textile industry brought prosperity to the town and region. The houses and workshops of the weavers, carders and dyers were built facing the gently flowing river.

On the far side washerwomen beat their laundry kneeling on little wooden stands. Today this trade has vanished or is continued in specialized factories, the old houses have been rebuilt, restored and are now private residences, with their colored façades, their verandas and bay windows that reflect the waters of the river.

LYON
ST JOHN'S CATHEDRAL

St Pothin came from Asia to bring Christianity to Lyon; he became the first bishop of the city and suffered martyrdom by lynching in 177 AD. His friend and disciple St Irenaeus, also from Asia, succeeded him. This was the first Christian community in Gaul.

St John's Cathedral was built a thousand years later. The surrounding area has grown but the church is still surrounded by a maze of little streets and squares. Started in the 12th, continued in the 13th, finished in the 14th centuries, this "primatial" cathedral has a romanesque sanctuary and side chapels, a gothic flat roofed nave and transepts and a pre-classical façade.

Archbishops of Lyon are "Primates of the Gauls": here two Councils were held, two Popes consecrated and King Henry IV of France married Marie de Medicis.

184

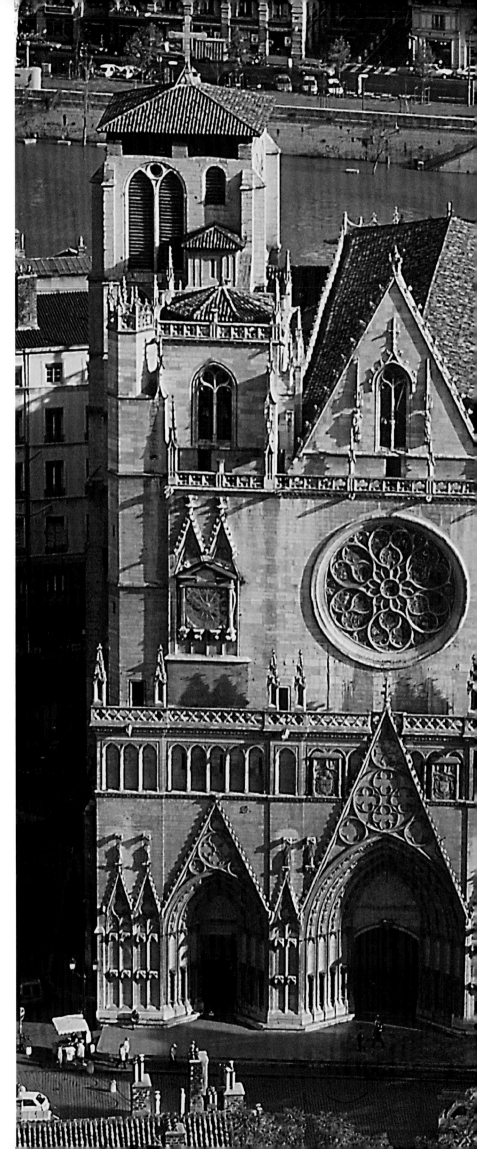

LYON
A TRABOULE

You only find them in Lyon! A "traboule" is a road running across main roads (Latin *trans-ambulare*, walk across), a short cut, making one's way between buildings... the way taken by those with local knowledge. They to go back to the 4th century when those living on the Fourvière and Croix-Rousse hills needed shortcuts through the lower city in order to get water from the Saône during dry weather.

Over the centuries the working population took over the area by the river and built the "traboules". Today they are being restored; three hundred and fifteen have been listed, more used by tourists and strollers than by busy citizens. Rue Saint-Jean is the busiest and most picturesque.

GRENOBLE
THE OLD TOWN

The same building as on the Place St-Jean in Lyon No. This picture was taken in Grenoble, and while Grenoble has no "traboules", it does have old neighborhoods that look exactly like those of Lyon. In the middle ages Grenoble was already an active business crossroads.

In the 12th century the Counts began calling themselves Dauphins, and Grenoble became the capital of the Dauphins: hence the title of Dauphiné used for today's province.

Dauphiné became part of France in 1349, when the Dauphin Humbert transferred all his possessions to the king in payment of his debts. The Gothic and Renaissance Palace of the Dauphins is today's law courts. In these ancient streets the Middle Ages are everywhere: the university dates from 1339, the former town hall, now the Stendhal Museum, from the 16th century, the cathedral from the 12th and 13th centuries and the church of St-André from the 13th.

Grenoble can be doubly proud: as a modern city and as one with a splendid past.

CIBOURE
THE HARBOR

Ciboure belongs to a part of the country where " four plus three make one", the motto of the Basque country which has Spanish provinces (Guipuzcoa, Biscay, Alava and Navarre) and French ones (Labourd, Lower Navarre and Soule). Ciboure is in Labourd, inside a magnificent bay, separated from Saint-Jean-de-Luz by the River Nivelle. Zubiru-Ciboure means "bridge-head" in Basque and shares the same history as its neighbor. The descendants of whale fishermen,

Newfoundland fishermen and pirates still live there. It has had illustrious guests - Louis XIV married the Infanta of Spain there - and unknown ones, notably pilgrims on their way to Santiago de Compostela. Amongst the fine, traditional houses of Ciboure, decorated with wooden panels and painted purple-red, one building stands out on the quays near St Vincent's Church. Its owner had business interests in Holland and built it in Dutch style in the 18th century. It is where Maurice Ravel was born. His mother was Basque and he often stayed in Ciboure. Painters, other composers and writers also loved this place.

HONFLEUR
LA LIEUTENANCE

Honfleur was a fortified town that played an important role in the Hundred Years' War. It was taken in 1346 by King Edward II of England, lost, retaken; it remained English until 1450.

La Lieutenance was first mentioned in the 11th century. It once formed part of a corner tower of the ramparts around the town; these have almost entirely disappeared. In the 16th century it was the "town chamber" where the inhabitants' council met. Above the building there was a belfry to sound the alarm.

In the Middle Ages the city had two gateways; the present Lieutenance incorporates what remains of one of them, the Caen Gateway: a ceiling arch, two towers and a niche in which has been placed a statue of the Blessed Virgin given to the town by the queen, Anne of Austria, in 1643. In 1684 Colbert ordered the construction of the old harbor. From that date, and up to the Revolution, the building was the official residence of the King's Lieutenant. Whence its name.

BASTIA
THE OLD PORT

First built between 1636 and 1666, the church of St John the Baptist was extended in the 18th century and became the largest in Corsica. Its handsome Gothic facade and two bell towers seem there to protect the old port, the cradle of the city's prosperity. It was here, in the 14th century, that the Genoans built the first fortifications, from which they could keep a watchful eye on the island of Elba and the coast of Tuscany.

Today's Bastia is the largest and most dynamic city in eastern Corsica, with its square, solid houses and their green, ocher or white shutters, its countless café terraces under their multicolored awnings, and its old quarters with their narrow alleys and tiny squares.

Bastia has kept, too, the two jetties of its old port; but, a sign of the times, the fishermen have gone, leaving the moorings to the yachts of those who go boating for pleasure. FOLLOWING PAGES

VILLAGES AND HAMLETS

CITIES AND VILLAGES

In those days Paris was called Lutetia and Lyon was Lugdunum. They were villages. They became cities. What's the difference? They will tell you that a village is small, a city is big, but the real difference is sociological, the social structures are not the same at all... In terms of numbers alone, pernickety civil servants have decided that a village is a place inhabited by less than 2000 inhabitants, what's more any house more than 200 yards away from the others is not part of the village... by this official calculation 33000 of the 36000 communes of France are villages.

But that is not the true differences at all: the first cities evolved between 4000 and 5000 years BC. They were in Mesopotamia and Egypt. The only reason they differed from the villages that had existed up to then, was that they no longer had a purely agricultural function; they were now centers of traditional industry and trade, but most significantly, they were also important from the point of view of religious practice, not to mention government. When one moves from village to city one comes nearer to the complexities of modern living, leaving behind the world of the farm for that of money and power.

RENEWAL IN THE MIDDLE AGES

French villages as we know them today began to appear in the Middle Ages. That appears late to us, so why the Middle Ages? The fall of the Roman Empire was followed by waves of invasions. The Germanic invasions were in the 3rd century, Barbarians came in the 5th; the Norsemen and the Arabs followed hot on their heels; the Hungarians arrived between the 8th and 10th centuries. So the Roman Empire was in fact followed by over five centuries of insecurity. Those years of instability had completely overthrown the traditional rural way of life. Since the conquest of Gaul by the Romans, this had revolved around villae, big agricultural businesses, with the owner's house, lodgings for servants and slaves, also farm buildings. The word village was forged from villa. Gaul had become France, but five hundred years of war and pillaging had wiped out the way the Romans had organized themselves socially and economically.

Hugues Capet came to the throne in 987 and put an end to political uncertainty, if not to war. Yet, to the modern eye, the size of his kingdom seems pathetic. The king would need to enlarge his tiny kingdom, make safe his insecure borders and eliminate his powerful rivals: rivals who were in fact often richer and more powerful than he was himself. In provincial France, people sought the double protection of the Lord and the lord, God and the local nobleman, faith and sword, priest and soldier.

194

They built their places of business, and consequently their homes, close to castle and church, the centers of military and religious power. The first villages were not of course built following any pre-established design; they evolved out of the need to survive. There was no town planning. Houses were built, as they were needed, of wood and of a mixture of clay and straw. Narrow, twisting lanes developed rather than streets. Farm animals used them, so they were winding and mucky. Occasionally a central channel drained off water.

In other cases, and with the passage of time this became more frequent, the founding of a village was carefully thought out beforehand. They looked for water: a spring, a stream or a river, a ford or a crossing point. Security was a major factor; a site should look down on approach roads. A wall or other fortification would defend the village. In the south, circular ramparts were the norm: inside the streets were laid out in concentric circles. This made the work of laying out the site much easier: contemporary plans show a rope turning around a central peg. A thousand years later modern town planners would invent the word circulade for these centers.

In the twelve hundreds, the Cathar faith spread throughout the southwest, to the great alarm of the Catholic Church: Simon de Montfort was put in charge of a merciless crusade and was ordered to rid the area of heresy. He was a fine organizer as well as a cruel soldier. He put the Languedoc to fire and the sword and built new-style villages for the new inhabitants. They had to sign a lease with the local lord or the priest; everything was pre-arranged: where the communal buildings should be, the shops, the dwelling houses, the number of families, the taxes they would pay, the exemptions they would enjoy, the corporation that would run the village. What was unusual about his organization was that the streets were laid out at right angles and organized, not around the church, but around the market square, which was surrounded by arcades where the stallholders would be sheltered from the sun when they laid out their wares. This model, or bastide, spread all over Aquitaine, particularly during the Hundred Years' War. Beaumont de Périgord 1272, Caillac 1280, Monpazier 1285, Hastingues 1289 etc. were English; Castillones 1259, Villeréal 1269, Monflanquin 1279 etc. were French. Both sides vied with each other to settle and protect their supporters. 90 circulades and 300 bastides still exist today, protected and preserved, visited and admired by thousands of tourists.

But in other parts of France the village stretched out on either side of a road, a valley or a stream. In the east the village street was bordered by long, thin strips of land. The houses were built of stone where there were local quarries, half-timbered where wood was plentiful. Soon the streets were being built wide enough for carts. Drains were developed for used water, a village laundry for the local housewives and a meeting hall for village business: progress was constant, even though lagging well behind the "modern" town planning practiced by the Romans.

THE BIRTH OF LOCAL GOVERNMENT

In the Middle Ages and under the later kings, villages were run by the parish; this would lead to many a political struggle in later centuries and indeed its fruits are still evident today. The church authorities kept the registers of baptisms, marriages and deaths, the local lord imposed order, and the villagers themselves had their say through the local town officers (consuls, jurats, capitouls, magistrats). These were either elected or nominated, generally for one year or two.

The Revolution would impose a single system: the Law of 14th December 1789, created 44000 communes instead of the old parishes. They were run by a mayor and a general council elected for two years, half the members were renewed each year. Only active citizens paying taxes amounting to 10 days' wages were electors. The council had two levels: office holders and council staff. Things have not changed much since: there are now 36000 communes and council members are elected for six years.

THE VILLAGE AND THE RHYTHM OF THE SEASONS

Village life was organized round farm life. The daily timetable was dictated by the sun. People got up early, did not sit up after dark; they took an afternoon nap when it was very hot. They wasted no time during plowing, harvest or grape picking; in winter they could relax a little, walk around, gossip with neighbors, before feeding animals, splitting wood or shoveling snow. Once or twice a week, neighboring country folk came into town to sell their produce at market: the streets and alleys were particularly lively on those days: cows, sheep or pigs on sale here, further on it was hens, geese or ducks; farmers' wives laid out freshly picked fruit and vegetables. Street entertainers of every sort went where the crowds were to earn a little money. The public houses were full all day, and sometimes all night too. Some of these markets achieved national, even international importance.

VILLAGE PLACE NAMES

Nineteenth century research into the study of place names shows how important nature and the countryside were in the development of villages.

Villages were often built on high ground: about a thousand place names have the element mont (mountain). This can stand alone (Mons, Mont), or with an adjective (Montaigu, Beaumont, Clermont, Montfort), or with somebody's name (Montbéliard, Montdidier). The Occitan word puy, pech or pey has the same meaning (Le Puy, Puylaurens, Puget). Occitan is an old language once widely spoken in the south of France; now in danger of dying out.

The village might be built in a valley: Laval, Valbonne, Vals, Vaux, Vaucresson, Levallois; or between two valleys: Entrevaux, Entraigues; or near a river (Latin rivus): Rieux, Rioux, Xonrupt; near a spring (L fons): Fontanges, Fontenay, Fontenelle, Fontevrault.

More importantly silva the forest has given us Selves, La Selve, Lasseube, Tresserve; the Gaulish word broglio (an enclosed wood) gave us Breuil, Le Breuil, Breil, Le Breil; sacred wood (L lucus) gave us Le Luc, Luc, Lacq, Lacanau, Lucmau, Lalucque. The French word bois (wood) gave Le Bois, Le Bois-Fleury, Frichebois. Trees also turn up in place names. Holly (L ilex aquifolium) inspired Aigrefeuille, Arfeuilles, Arpheuilles; the alder (Fr aulne) Lannoy, Launay, Aulnoye; the hazel (Fr noisetier, avelinier or coudrier) Lavelanet, Averan, Coudray, Corroy; boxwood (Fr buis) La Boissière, Buissières, Bruxières; the chestnut (Fr châtaignier) inspired La Châtaigneraie, Châtenoy, Castanet, Castagnède; the beech (L fagus) Faux, Fay, La Fage, La

Fayette; bracken (Fr fougère) gave us Feugères, Fougères, Fougerolles; the ash (Fr frêne) gave Fresnay, Fresnoy, Fraisse; the lime tree (Fr tilleul) inspired Tilly, le Theil, Thieux; the aspen (Fr tremble) La Tremblade; the oak (Fr chêne) Chasnais, Chasseneuil, Chaignes, Chaignay, Le Chesne, Beau-Chesne. Of course place names use the word ville, which came from the Latin word villa (a country estate), before it got its modern meaning: Villebois, Belleville, Villars, Villiers, Villersexel, Aubervilliers. The Latin vicus (estate) and vicinus (neighborhood) gave us Vic, Vicq, Neuvic, Le Vésinet. These are but a few examples. Borrowings from religious language were frequent, as were trade terms, not to mention borrowings from Breton, Occitan, Basque and Germanic sources.

THE SCARS OF HISTORY

More than anything else the great movements of history have, throughout the ages, left their mark on local activity. Village names resound in the great events and upheavals of wider history. Villages pillaged by medieval gangs, torn apart by religious strife in the 16th and 17th centuries, ravaged by the military adventures of Louis XIV or Napoleon; bled dry by 20th century conscription, razed to the ground by modern warfare. But we must also remember villages on the medieval pilgrimage route to Santiago de Compostela, villages voting for the Republic in 1848, villages now endowed with a school following the reforms of Jules Ferry in 1881-82; villages where, on the war memorials, one can read the cost in blood to the nation.

In the 17th century, 90% of the population lived in the countryside. The villagers were country folk, making a living from the land, with a few professionals and shopkeepers mixed in. Later developments in agriculture, particularly mechanization, attracted salesmen, veterinary surgeons and owners of hardware businesses, who set up shop in opposition to the traditional blacksmith. Then what we now call the consumer society brought much greater spending power, but also demanded much wider choice. In the 20th century villages declined, many died. Those that survived found new ways of making a living: holiday villages, skiing villages, workers' villages and fishing villages. Or else they were able to put new structures in place: holiday housing, new factories, tourism and heritage. Elsewhere a new awareness of nature and the environment has brought a new population back to the countryside: city people fed up with various forms of urban violence and pollution. In the race for survival, notoriety or development, three types of village have a special advantage: those connected to an important historical event, those where a local figure has become famous on the national or international stage and those which produce an incomparable product.

Who would have heard of Agincourt, a small village in the Pas-de-Calais, if, on the 25th October 1415, English archers had not annihilated the fine flower of the French nobility there? Who would know anything about Varennes-en-Argonne if King Louis XVI and his family had not been arrested there as they fled from Paris and Revolution? Or what about Sainte-Mère-Église in Normandy, the first European town liberated by American paratroopers, a few hours before the beach landings, on the 6th June 1944? Would anybody have heard of Oradour-sur-Glane, in Haute-Vienne, had it not been the scene of a Nazi atrocity when the whole population, women, old people and children included, were killed by the SS das Reich division on 10th June 1944?

Elsewhere a famous person from the locality has given new life to a village. Nohant, six miles from La Châtre, was the country retreat of George Sand and the rural setting for all her novels. The name of Brigitte Bardot attracts the Paris glitterati, and much else besides, to Saint-Tropez, a little port hidden in a bend of the Mediterranean coast.

In other cases a traditional activity and a product of incomparable quality ensure income and renown: Baccarat, Saint-Émilion, Sauternes, Camembert, Livarot. Other villages have started from scratch: La Gascilly in Brittany has benefited from the dynamism of local son Yves Rocher. Often what counts is how they promote some exceptional element of heritage: an ancient monument, an abbey, church or castle. Would Chenonceau be famous if the two rivals Diane de Poitiers and Catherine de Medicis had not built a masterpiece over the waters of the River Cher?

Thousands of villages have lost their raison d'être in farming but, because they possess an exceptional treasure, have determined to preserve it and make the most of it. Signs of the times, but welcome signs!

GASTRONOMICAL MAP OF FRANCE

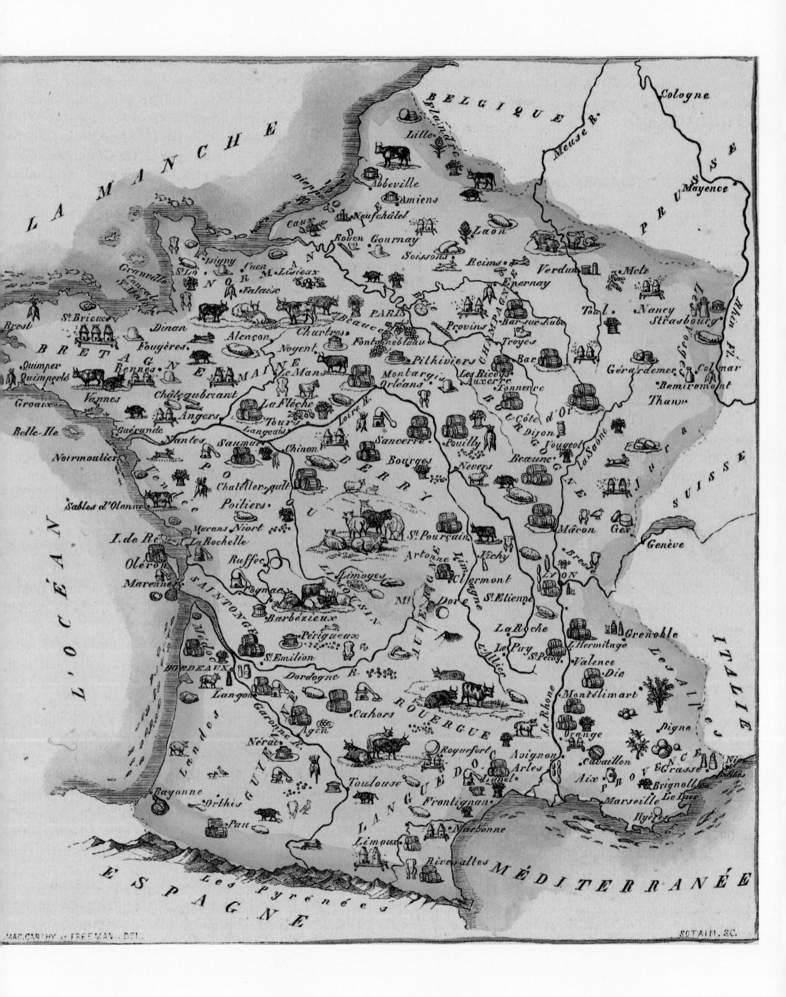

CHAMPAGNE

THE MOËT
ET CHANDON BUILDING

Vines have been a tradition in Champagne since the time of the Romans (4th century), and then the clergy took over (the bishops of Reims and of Chalons). Mention of "Champagne wines" was first made in the reign of Henry IV. The locals did not approve, for to them the word "champagne" meant infertile ground. The word would, however, make many fortunes.

Dom Pérignon (1638-1715, and consequently an exact contemporary of Louis XIV) was the monk responsible for the vineyards, presses and cellars of the

Benedictine Abbey of Hautvilliers, and held to be the inventor of champagne. That's an exaggeration, for before him they bottled champagne immediately without allowing it to age in casks. Unlike Bordeaux, it deteriorates with age. What's more, they used to add sugar and aromatic spices; but the corks often popped or the bottles exploded, the wine had become fizzy!

Dom Pérignon's stroke of genius was to find a way to allow the wine to age in the bottle, and to mix wines made from different grapes to achieve a grace of taste and reliable quality, while getting rid of the need for additives. He also invented the cork stopper and the means of attaching it to the bottle.

MOUTHIER-HAUTE-PIERRE

CHERRY BLOSSOMS

A few miles from the Swiss border, at the northeastern tip of Franche-Comté, the Loue River surges up out of the ground in a copious spring and makes an impressive descent (it drops 750 feet in 12 miles), hollowing out its bed in the chalky plateau of the Jura mountains as it flows east from Dole before joining the River Doubs.

Up near the source an abrupt cliff face 3000 feet high looks down on wooded gorges: it's called Haute Pierre. About 800 AD Benedictine monks built a priory at the foot of this enormous rock on the right bank of the Loue,

the one facing the sun. The mustier or monastery gave its name to the village, which, over the years, grew up nearby. The church, together with the surrounding upper village, dates from the 16th century, as does the bridge across the Loue in the lower village. The local small industries: sawmills, tanning, oil pressing were started in the 18th century.

Grapes and cherries are grown locally; the village is renowned for its cherries; traditionally Marsotte, but these are disappearing, also Catelle and Faux-vache.

The trees flower in April, the cherries are picked in July. The fruit are distilled to produce kirsch, "the best kirsch available", say the locals.

203

TURCKHEIM
THE TOWN HALL
AND ST ANNE'S CHURCH

Turckheim is a charming village at the entrance to the Fecht valley in Alsace, half way between Colmar in the east and Le Grand Hohneck in the west. The town had been lived in since Roman times, it appears for the first time on the Charter of Wissembourg in 743. It was part of lands held by the lords of Turckheim, a family that died out in the 15th century. Turckheim then became a member of the Decapolis, an alliance of ten free Alsatian cities, a league that would be dissolved in 1679.

Three gateways survive from the old town wall of 1315. The Town Hall (seen here) was built in 1598, that is where the Magistrat, the body composed of four governors and six bourgeois with responsibility for administering the town, met. Nearby, the church of St Anne, built in neo-classical style on the site of an old romanesque church (the bell tower still exists), was first of all dedicated to the Blessed Virgin and later to her mother, St Anne. Why the change? Simply to distinguish it from the Trois-Épis pilgrimage that leads the faithful every year to the Trois-Épis (three heads of corn) chapel, just above the village. This chapel is dedicated to the Virgin Mary who has performed several miracles there.

The top of the five-storied bell tower is crowned with the symbol of Alsace winemakers: a gilded wine barrel, with above that, a weathervane in the shape of a star.

EGUISHEIM

HALF TIMBERED HOUSES AND GERANIUMS

The village of Eguisheim gets its name from a distant founder, Egeno, or Egino, or even Egerhard, who, about 720 AD, restored the modest castle in the center of what was then a little town. In the 13th century, the present octagonal castle was built on the ruins of the earlier building.

The streets were built around it over the centuries, in three concentric circles which, when seen from the sky, make the village look like a tennis racket or a football. The village's unique charm comes from the half-timbered houses with oriel (glassed in balconies) windows.

These "tithe" houses (they were paid for by the payment of a tithe) or wine growers' houses date from the 16th and 17th centuries. It also comes from the work that the householders put into decorating their balconies, their house fronts, even their footpaths with flowers. It is more than a flower-decorated village; it is a village that is itself a garden.

Three castles look down over the village from a spur in the Vosges. They are in fact three dungeons surviving from the split up of the princely residence of the Egerhard family; today they reign over little more than a few ruins, but they do it in style! Eguisheim saw the birth, in 1002, of the future Pope Leo IX, the first great reformer of the Roman church.

THE VOSGES
A WINTER FOREST SCENE

Life is hard in the Vosges. The winters are cold; the temperature remains below zero for 150 days out of 365. Violent winds often sweep across the rounded tops of the mountains

The people are like the land: used to harsh forest work; capable of bringing in a ton of wood in a single trip on a *schlitte* (a sledge dragged along a log pathway)…though in fact this way of doing things has almost died out, except for tourist demonstrations… But at the same time the land has a certain gentleness: the mountains are round, there is scarcely a steep slope, that's why they are called ballons (footballs), though it has to be said that the word comes originally from a Germanic dialect. What is more, the beech and fir, which go to make up most of the forest, do not stop the light, as oak and other broad-leaved trees do, they filter it.

And when it snows on the trees, as in the photo, the ground and the air take on a bluish, pastel glow, the branches drip with icy lacework, and the fir trunks stand out black and stiff in this peaceful universe.

208

IN THE NORTH
A COUNTRY COTTAGE

The oldest and most frequent style of building out in the country is (or was) the *longère*.

We are at the bottom of the architectural ladder: the first *longères* were no more than one step up from a hut.

By definition a *longère* was a long narrow house, rectangular, one level only. Built for small holders, laborers, casual workers, tenants, craftsmen and handymen. The single room was divided by a half partition to separate the animals' section from where the humans lived.

210

Later a cow house was added on to the gable end, and the longère was given a fireplace and chimney. This second space was generally a sign of improved financial conditions. *Longères* were built in all areas of France, but were the preferred style for those living along the Atlantic and English Channel coasts. Often huddled behind a dune, a big rock or a clump of pine trees, the longère sheltered from the caprices of the wind: sudden gusts off the sea.

In the 19th century they started building "rich *longères*" (two words which, up to then, were contradictions), these were never occupied by a farmer or a fisherman, but by members of the middle classes. Today's citizens, anxious to buy a country cottage, snatch them up avidly.

VEULES-LES-ROSES

THE VILLAGE

The pains of love made Veules famous. It hadn't yet been named Veules-les-Roses. Anaïs Aubert was an actress in the Comédie Française and suffered greatly when she was let down by her lover. She withdrew to this village where she found peace and renewed interest in life. She made it fashionable in artistic and literary circles in Paris in a typically 19th century way.

Veules had first become prosperous from fishing in the reign of Philip the Fair. After the Wars of Religion, weavers had come here; they washed wool and crushed flax in the waters of the Veules River. Encouraged by Anaïs Aubert, intellectuals arrived, then summer holidaymakers.

Looking at the village today you can see the different stages of its development. It is a succession of harmonious buildings, fishermen's houses, cottages, farms, mills, laundry basins, half-timbered walls, thatched roofs, tidy villas covered with roses, flower-filled gardens, and threading its way between these picturesque buildings, the River Veules, the smallest river in France.
PREVIOUS PAGES

VILLEQUIER

THE PRESBYTERY

Charles Vacquerie was twenty-six when, on the 15th February 1843, he married nineteen-year-old Léopoldine, the daughter of the poet Victor Hugo. Six months later, on the 4th September, shortly after midday, with their uncle Pierre and their young nephew Arthur, they got into a boat to return to Villequier from Caudebec-en-Caux. A sudden gust of wind overturned the craft and the four passengers were drowned. Victor Hugo only learned the news five days later and suffered deep pain.

The Vacqueries' house in Villequier was bought by the county authority of Seine-Maritime as a Victor Hugo museum. It is a big comfortable middle class house, typical of this region.

A short distance away, right beside the church, the half-timbered presbytery is also typical of Normandy.

LYONS-LA-FORÊT
HALF-TIMBERED HOUSES

Lyons-la-Forêt is considered to be one of the most beautiful villages in France. Its main square is lined with half-timbered houses that set off the old market building. It is the most famous square in Normandy and much visited by the inhabitants of the Ile de France.

Across the road, rue de l'Enfer (Hell Street) slopes gently down into the forest. In the distance you can see an elegant manor house, its roof decorated with

somewhat crooked dormer windows. The nearby lanes, the banks of the Lieure, the Lyons forest with its beech trees, all call out to the country walker. The woods are full of game and were once favorite hunting grounds for the Dukes of Normandy and other local lords.

A legend recalls that one of them, Arthus, was so carried away by his passion that he broke the rules and hunted a stag on Good Friday. He was condemned to pursue it for all eternity. The legend goes further: any one who sees his ghost will suffer the same fate.

CONCARNEAU
THE MOROS
ESTUARY

The Moros is a little river, barely ten miles long, but flows, after describing a magnificent arc, into Concarneau bay. It is shared by countryside and sea. Here we see a tiny island, round, healthy and green. But the river suddenly widens into a ria and laps against the sides of fishing boats anchored in the "ville-close", a medieval, fortified island in the middle of the bay, then it rubs against the yachts in the southern harbor.

On one bank of the Moros a manor house nestles among the trees; in the seventeenth century it belonged to the lieutenant general of the King's Navy, Abraham Dusquesne (he was never made Admiral or Marshal… because he was a Protestant!) He lived here for ten years until his marriage and then divided his time between Moros, Paris and Brest. They say that Felix Youssoupov, who had murdered the mystic Rasputin, the favorite of the Tsar and Tsarina Alexandra, also lived here. Youssoupov was never prosecuted and lived in France: a relative owned Kériolet Castle in Concarneau.

THE POITOU
MARSHES
GREEN VENICE

The house with blue shutters is by far the most famous in Green Venice, as this flood-prone part of the Poitou marshes is called. It is between Niort and the sea and called the wet marsh, as opposed to the dry marsh, which is protected by dikes all along the shore.

Here everything is in fact green: the trees (ash and clipped willow), the grasses, even the water, which is everywhere covered in a thick blanket of duckweed. This marsh, which has been patiently developed over the years since the 12th century, has grown into an inextricable tangle of water courses, canals, rivulets, ditches; it is crisscrossed by boats with no keels called plattes (locally pronounced piattes) steered by a pigouille (boathook) or a palle (paddle).

The house with blue shutters stands in splendid isolation on the banks of the Sèvre Niortaise, a few miles from Coulon, the "capital" of this expanse of water and greenness. FOLLOWING PAGES

NOHANT-VIC
THE HOUSE
OF GEORGE SAND

This village in the Berry was where Aurore Dupin, Baronness Dudevant grew up and where she lived for much of her life. The author of *Consuelo*, *La Mare au Diable* and *La Petite Fadette* made her mark with tales set in the country, but impregnated with an idealism borrowed from Rousseau, together with a hint of socialism. She was also famous for the freedom of her lifestyle. She was divorced, wore trousers and a man's hat.

222

The "good woman of Nohant" welcomed many of the artists of her day to her large 18th century countryseat surrounded by the garden she loved to tend. Nohant "Castle" is not really a castle but a big middle-class house, called castle because George Sand lived there. Madame Dupin de Franceuil, natural daughter of Marshal de Saxe and grandmother of "the good woman of Nohant" had bought it in 1793. It was she who built the main staircase and planted the gardens and orchard. She took in her granddaughter when the latter was only four. George Sand inherited the "castle" in 1821.

SAINT-PIERRE DE MAILLÉ
THE GARTEMPE

The Gartempe rises near Guéret in the Creuse region, some 2000 feet above sea level. In the early part of its course it flows swiftly, heading west through restless hills, green countryside, flower decked villages, then suddenly heads north, changes into a tumultuous torrent as it goes through the Gates of Hell (Portes de l'Enfer), rushes east from Poitiers and Châtellerault before joining the Creuse at La Roche-Posay. Much calmer in its last few miles, it flows

through a number of villages with historical associations. These are Montmorillon, with its curious 11th century Octagon and its 12th century houses; Pindray and the Pruniers castle, a 14th century stronghold; Angles-sur-l'Anglin, with its sculptures from 15,000 BC and its medieval castle; Saint-Savin, with its Romanesque abbey and 11th century frescoes; Saint-Pierre-de-Maillé, where prehistoric remains, a dolmen, a cave used about 30,000 BC, Roman remains, a road, pillars, ruins, classical architecture, the castle of Puygirault, modern sport with rock climbing sites all sit cheek by jowl.

COLLONGES-LA-ROUGE

THE SANDSTONE TOWN

Colonges is between the Vézère and the Dordogne, and built of sandstone: hence its name. It is surrounded by vineyards, with forests of walnut and chestnut trees. This town in Corrèze has fine residences and manor houses built at the time of the Renaissance by the agents of the powerful Viscount of Turenne, whose castle is nearby.

Collonges had a defensive role in the Wars of Religion, as may be seen from the romanesque church's square tower.

Sculptors from Toulouse who worked there in the Middle Ages also had a hand in the building of the Abbey of Beaulieu-sur-Dordogne, one of the glories of medieval art. The old oven used by the inhabitants is still within its fine covered market.

Turrets, watchtowers, mullioned windows, pepper-boxes, sculpted faces, attic rooms and vines climbing across the façades: the streets of Collonges are a delight. We meet the same red sandstone in the castle at Castelnau-Bretenoux, "blood-colored stone lace", according to Pierre Loti, or again in the Rouergue in Rodez cathedral.

TERRASSON-LAVILLEDIEU

THE BRIDGE

Trick question: in what village would you find this old bridge? A map published before 1963 gives you La Villedieu. On 1st January 1963 the commune merged with its neighbor Terrasson.

On more recent maps you find Terrasson-La-Villedieu. But on the 25th December 1997 the name was officially changed. And on most recent maps you should find Terrasson-Lavilledieu, if the cartographers have been doing their job properly! But look in a guidebook and you may find, "gateway to Black Périgord".

Terrsasson-Lavilledieu is in effect a most picturesque village in the Dordogne, clinging to the banks of the Vézère, slightly upstream from Lascaux. It already existed in Roman times, earlier indeed, we believe, but there is no proof! Its first Abbey was founded in the 6th century.

Burials from the Merovigian period have been found. In the Middle Ages they built wood paneled houses there and a maze of picturesque streets, the Renaissance brought elegant stone houses. In the 12th century they built a superbly arched bridge across the Vézère. The village experienced the Hundred Years' War, the Wars of Religion, paid the cost of Resistance in 1944. Today it watches, not without satisfaction, even when they are a bit noisy, armies of tourists.

LA ROQUE-GAGEAC
THE VALLEY

A broad, gentle river, with sparkling water slipping between clumps of poplars, ash and beech, a boat drifting beneath the foliage, between houses roofed with stone shingles, which look out over well-watered and lush fields. We are in peaceful Périgord.

The Dordogne lazily waters a fertile plain. But the Périgord was not always calm, not even here.

We need not go back to pre-historic times, although humans had by then arrived, just to the Middle Ages, to the Viking invasions, the English occupation, to the Hundred Years' war, to the Wars of Religion. There was a lot of fighting; they had to build a lot of fortresses.

The region bristles with enormous strongholds. The one from which this photo was taken is one of the most unusual: it is a troglodyte or cave fortress, tunneled into the cliff face; a gaping opening in the rock provides a natural terrace and covering. You have to climb up to it. An underground spring, loopholes, a secret exit all made the fort invulnerable. Never once in the course of its history did it fall into enemy hands, no matter who they were.

The boat in the river is a replica of a 17th or 18th century *gabarre*. These were flat-bottomed boats with oars, but equipped also with a sail. They were heavy and slow, but capable of going out to sea. They were used for transporting goods up until the arrival of the railways. Today they are used for tourist trips.

MARQUÈZE
A HENHOUSE

In the 19th century in the Landes region, shepherds got up on stilts to watch their sheep hidden in the long grass. The land was marshy; the systematic planting of vegetation capable of stabilizing the sands had just begun. The inhabitants were still being killed by malaria, the houses being engulfed by the shifting dunes.

The locals cut gashes into the pine trees to allow the red gold flow out; the women tended their vegetable gardens, the men tended the forest.

232

They raised pigs, oxen to pull the heavy carts, mules because it was the best animal for the sandy roads (Napoleon III had tried in vain to import camels…); they raised ducks for duck confit and foie gras, hens who retired every night into raised henhouses like this one: foxes could not get in and the louvered floors allowed them to collect the manure.

All these elements of local life and work are illustrated in the ecological museum of Marquèze in the heart of the Landes region, where our photograph was taken. There you can see them tapping the pine trees, shearing sheep, cooking, cutting up ducks, and admire one of the best preserved sites in the region.

LAUZERTE
A DOVECOTE

Medieval laws were meticulous about dovecotes. One's rights certainly varied from place to place and from period to period; but the theory was stable. Only a lord could build a dovecote, and the number of niches provided depended on the extent of his lands.

Why were they more concerned about where pigeons lived than about cows, horses or sheep? No explanation is convincing though the succulence of their meat, the quality of their droppings or their ability to carry messages have all been suggested. We can but marvel at the care, artistry even, put into the building of some dovecotes.

The pillars protected the pigeons from climbing animals, the tops of the pillars from snakes, the small openings to the niches from birds of prey. Everything else: skylights, half-timbering of the buildings and embellishments were for display!

AUVILLAR
THE COVERED MARKET

Between Moissac and Valence d'Agen, in Tarn-et-Garonne, Auvillar is perched above a majestic bend in the Garonne. On the bank the river port, on the hill the village.

When was this beautiful village established? In Roman times doubtless, for numerous remains have been found, notably mosaics. The public laundry and underground passages date from the Middle Ages, the church is 12th century and the tower was built in the Sun-King's reign. But its most curious feature is the medieval triangular marketplace, with wood paneled, corbeled houses and other 17th and 18th century buildings. In the middle of this triangular area, the circular covered market is just as unusual. It has a central area, a sort of round tower with semi circular arches; this is surrounded by a circular gallery on Tuscan pillars. It is a relatively recent building: 1824. It was built on the site of an even earlier covered market.

You can still see vessels for measuring grain. There are both metal ones dating from the early 19th century or ones carved in stone from earlier centuries.

FOLLOWING PAGES

SAUVETERRE-DE-ROUERGUE

THE BASTIDE

It is 1271. It has been a difficult year since Phillip III, the Bold succeed the great king, St Louis. That year his uncle, Alphonse de Poitiers, Count of Toulouse, died; the king seized the county, which now came under the authority of the crown. But he had to impose royal authority over a turbulent province troubled by the willfulness of local lords, with unsafe roads and roaming brigands. Philip the Bold named William of Vienne and Macon seneschal of the Rouergue (modern Aveyron) and ordered him to build a new fortified town in Sauveterre; thus the inhabitants would be protected and have a charter allowing them numerous liberties.

The ground plan of the town was simple and effective. At the center a rectangular bastide (town layout frequent in the southwest), built apparently on the site of an old feudal castle. The square was two hundred feet by one hundred and thirty; in the local dialect it was a *chitats* (pronounce every single letter!); all around are magnificent arcades, over which wood paneled houses are built. A significant detail in all bastides is that the church is away from the central square. Around the square the town is laid out like a chessboard, the streets are all at right angles; a curtain wall pierced by four gates surrounds it.

Thanks to tornals, mills built over nearby water courses for sharpening and grinding, Sauveterre-de-Rouergue will long be the knife-making capital of France, before being dethroned by another local town: Laguiole.

239

IN THE CÉVENNES
SHEEP

Sheep, like chestnuts, are an integral part of the history and economy of the Cévennes. It was from ancient times the route taken when moving flocks up to high summer pasture. They came from the Languedoc and headed for La Margeride and Aubrac. They traveled in flocks of several hundred, using roads called drailles, which they had themselves created, avoiding valleys and keeping to the heights, following instinct.

Shepherds improved these drailles, building across gorges and crevices the shale sheep-bridges that now delight ramblers. Many types of economic activity are based on sheep: shepherds, cheese makers, tanners (here called basanes), and sheep dealers. But transhumance is no longer what it was.

In 1700 there were 100,000 sheep on Mount Lozère: 10,000 only in 1980. Much has been done since to protect traveling flocks; today their numbers are estimated at between fifteen and twenty thousand animals. PREVIOUS PAGES

SAINT-CIRQ-LAPOPIE

Down below, the river Lot is impatient to get to the sea, lapping up against the remains of ports, locks and towpaths, nostalgic remains of bygone times when trade in hides, caldrons and wooden molds for taps and buttons all used the river for transport. Three hundred feet above the gorges, clinging to the rocky slope, the medieval village proudly displays its stone houses with wooden panels; the beautiful tile roofs are steeply sloped. The top of the village is dominated by the 15th century church, a lordly building with its square keep, flanked by turrets and with a romanesque apse. Higher still rise the ruins of a castle, or rather three castles, which defended the site in the 13th and 14th centuries. Henry IV destroyed it during the Wars of Religion, when half the village was Catholic, the other half Huguenot. Saint-Cirq Lapopie has been justly named the most beautiful village in the Quercy region.

SAORGE
THE VILLAGE

As a village it would take your breath away, but also make you giddy! Saorge is built into the rock, like an amphitheater overlooking the sheer gorges of the Roya River.

The streets are narrow, sometimes very steep, some in steps, laid out in an impenetrable maze. At the top, the Franciscan convent displays its baroque façade; at the very bottom, the romanesque tower of the church of the Madonna del Poggio makes you think you are in Lombardy. Half ways up are other churches, three chapels of a 17th century Penitent confraternity.

From a distance the village seems to hang impressively above the valley. Its interlacing of blue mauve roofs of stone or many-colored varnished tiles, its white walls all gleam in the sun.

In the Middle Ages Saorge was called "the bolt of the Roya" and was protected by three fortresses. It was held to be impregnable and indeed wasn't captured until 1794. Masséna had just been promoted general when he succeeded, thus opening Napoleon's way to the Piedmont two years later.

PREVIOUS PAGES

FONTVIEILLE
THE WINDMILL OF ALPHONSE DAUDET

"It was a windmill for grinding flour, sitting in the Rhône valley, right in the heart of Provence, on a wooded slope covered in pine and oak… All week long what a pleasure to listen to the noise of the sails and to get the warm smell of ground wheat which floats around mills."

That was how Alphonse Daudet, the author of *"Letters from my Windmill"* described the little corner of Provence he loved so well. However he didn't write his letters here but in Paris, where he was a teacher's assistant. He wasn't happy in the capital; his heart and soul belonged in Fontvielle. He had become friendly with the Ambroy brothers, who lived in the castle.

He visited them as often as possible and when not with them wandered in this land of stones, pine trees, olive trees and green oak set against the background of the Baux valley and the foothills of the Alps. He bought the mill. Back in Paris he could smell again the thyme and lavender, hear the sound of the local language, the warmth of the southern accent and, imagining himself back there, took up his pen.

INDEX

248

BIBLIOGRAPHY

BATAILLE Georges, La peinture préhistorique, Skira, 1 955.

BUSSELLE Michaël., L'art roman, Könemann, 1999.

BEDNORZ A. Toman Discovering the Villages of France, Arcade Pub, 1994.

BRAUDEL Fernand, L'identité de la France, Arthaud Flammarion, 1986.

CASTIEAU Thérèse, L'art roman, Flammarion, 1998.

CASTELOT André, DECAUX Alain, Dictionnaire de l'Histoire de France, Perrin, 1981.

COLLECTIF, Les plus beaux villages de France, Reader's Digest 2005

COLLECTIF, Les plus beaux châteaux de France, Reader's Digest 2004

CRANSTON LARNED Walter, Churches and Castles of Medieval France, Oxford Press, 2004

DECKER Michel de, Les Grandes Heures de la Normandie, Perrin, 1988.

DUBY Georges, L'Europe au Moyen Age, Flammarion, 1981.

DUBY Georges, Fondements d'un nouvel humanisme, Skira, 1966.

DURLIAT Marcel, L'art roman, Citadelles et Mazenod, 1989.

ERLANDE BRANDEBOURG Alain, L'art gothique, Citadelles et Mazenod, 1989.

FABRE Gabrielle/VARAGNAC André, L'art gaulois, Zodiaque, 1964.

GARNOT Benoît, Les villes en France aux XVIᵉ/XVIIᵉ/XVIIIᵉ siècles, Ophrys 1998

GAXOTTE Pierre, Histoire des Français, Fayard, 1951.

JOUVE Anne-Marie/STRAGIOTTI FABRIES, La France des villes, Breal 2000

KIRCHHOFF Elisabeth, Histoire de France, Molière, 1994.

KIRCHHOFF Elisabeth, Rois et Reines de France, Molière, 1997.

LE ROY LADURIE Emmanuel, Histoire des paysans français, Seuil, 2002.

LORBLANCHET Michel, La naissance de l'art Genèse de l'art préhistorique, Errance, 1999.

MELCHIOR BONNET Christian (sous la direction de), Le grand livre de l'Histoire de France, Tallandier, 1980.

MESQUI Jean, Châteaux fort et fortifications en France, Flammarion 1997

MINNE SEVE/KERGALL, La France romane et gothique, Saint André des arts éditions, 2002.

MOLLAT Michel, Genèse médiévale de la France moderne, Arthaud, 1970.

MONNIER Jean Laurent, Les hommes de la préhistoire, Ouest France, 2002.

MOURIES Nathalie, Guide des villages de charme en France, Rivages 2005

MUMFORD Lewis, La cité à travers l'Histoire, Seuil, 1964.

OUDOIRE Jean-Marie, Cathédrales de France, Minerva 2001

PRACHE Anne, Initiation à l'art roman, architecture et sculpture, Zodiaque, 2002.

Préhistoire et antiquité, collectif, Gründ, 2000.

SAUPIN Guy, Les villes en France à l'époque moderne, Belin 2002

STAROBINSKI Jean, L'invention de la liberté, Skira, 1964.

TAINE Hippolyte, Les origines de la France contemporaine, 1876.

TILLINAC Denis, Le venin de la mélancolie, La Table Ronde, 2005.

TRILL0UX Paul, Le guide de l'art roman, Dervy, 1999.

TZONIS A/LEFAIVRE L. BILODEAU, Le classicisme en architecture, Dunod, 1993.

TULARD Jean, Le pouvoir de la rue, in Enquête sur l'histoire, ed. Société EC2M.

WOOLF Greg, Becoming Roman: the Origins of Provincial Civilization in Gaul, Cambridge University Press, 2004.

ZERNER Henri, L'art de la Renaissance en France, l'invention du classicisme, Flammarion, 2002.

All rights reserved.
© Molière, 2005
ISBN: 2-84790-084-5
Printed and bound in China

Photographic credit: P. Boussier: 10, 30/31, 56/57, 59, 70/71, 98/99, 110/111, 120/121, 128/129, 130/131, 132/133, 140/141, 144/145, 148/149, 150/151, 162/163, 172/173, 176/177, 191, 206/207, 216/217, 220/221, 224/225. Hervé Champollion: 1, 26/27, 32/33, 34/35, 36/37, 40/41, 46, 47, 48/49, 50/51, 53, 54/55, 56-57, 60/61, 62/63, 64/65, 67, 74/75, 76/77, 83, 96/97, 112/113, 116/117, 118/119, 122/123, 126/127, 142/143, 152/153, 160/161, 168/169, 174/175, 178/179, 180/181, 184/185, 186, 187, 219. Christophe Lefébure: 45. Dominique Repérant: 21, 22/23, 25, 28/29, 38/39, 42/43, 68/69, 73, 78/79, 80/81, 84/85, 86/87, 100/101, 102/103, 104/105, 106/107, 108/109, 124/125, 134/135, 136/137, 138/139, 146/147, 164/165, 167, 170/171, 182/183, 188/189, 192/193, 200/201, 202/203, 204/205, 208/209, 210/211, 214/215, 212/213, 215, 222/223, 226/227, 228/229, 230/231, 232/233, 235, 236/237, 238/239, 240/241, 243. D.R.: 12/13, 19/20, 94/95, 114/115, 252/253. Collaboration: F. B. S.B.

GRANDE Excesu BRETAGNE Dou

La Manche ou le Canal

la Hogue

Aldernay I.

Ro

Guernsey I.

Jersey I.

Caën

NORMANDIE

Alançon

St Malo

BRETAGNE

MAINE

Brest

Rennes

Man

Quimper

Port Louis

Nantes

Anger

Blou

Tours

Bellisle

Loire R.

Noirmoutier

Poitiers

POICTOU

Mer

Sables D'olone

la Rochelle

Isle De Rhé

Isle D'oleron

Oceane

Saintes

Dordonne R.

Perigeu

Tour de Cordouan

Bordeaux

GUIEN NE

Agen

GASCOGNE

Bayonne

Pau

Auch

Bearn

Garon

Oviedo

St Andre Bilboa

ESPAGN

St Bertrand

Po

Lion

Lieues de France

Pampl